THIS JOURNAL
BELONGS TO:

....

-&-

....

THE

US

JOURNAL

A Questionnaire
Keepsake *for* Couples

· · · · ·

FALL RIVER PRESS

New York

FALL RIVER PRESS

New York

An Imprint of Sterling Publishing Co., Inc.

FALL RIVER PRESS and the distinctive Fall River Press logo are registered
trademarks of Barnes & Noble, Inc.

Original text © 2007 Hollan Publishing, Inc.
New text © 2020 Union Square & Co., LLC.

This 2023 edition printed for Barnes & Noble, Inc. by Union Square & Co., LLC.

ISBN 978-1-4351-7325-5

Printed in China

2 4 6 8 10 9 7 5 3

unionsquareandco.com

Original text by Ali Davis
New text by Lindsay Herman
Interior design by Scott Russo
Cover design by Elizabeth Lindy

Floral background pattern on cover and throughout:
Hudyma Natallia/Shutterstock.com
Engraved heart lock on cover and throughout:
lestyan/Shutterstock.com

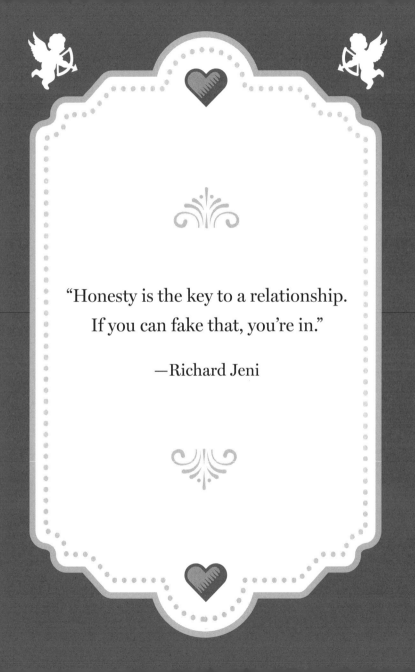

"Honesty is the key to a relationship.
If you can fake that, you're in."

—Richard Jeni

CONTENTS

Introduction

INTRODUCTION

"Love looks not with the eyes but with the mind."
—Shakespeare, *A Midsummer Night's Dream* (I, I, 234)

If you want the kind of love that Shakespeare writes about—the kind that runs deeper than the flesh and satisfies you in ways you never imagined—then it's time to bare all! Communication and honesty are the keys to a healthy relationship, whether you're coming clean with your significant other or simply with yourself. It's time to start asking some difficult questions: What do *I* really want in a relationship? How can I make the relationship I'm in more satisfying? What do I need from my partner?

The better you know yourself and how you want (make that *need*) to be loved, the better your love life will be. The more you know about your partner and your partner's needs, and the more you speak openly and honestly about desires, frustrations, expectations, and dreams, the greater your chances for an ever-growing, lasting love.

Whether you're a new couple just getting to know each other or old-timers in the romance department, *The Us Journal* offers an opportunity to step out of your daily routine and connect with one another in a meaningful way. It's filled with hundreds of leading questions that force you to look inward and let your deepest desires be known. Answer the questions together for a shared journaling exercise sure to spark conversation and bring a whole new level of understanding and satisfaction to your relationship.

All questions provide space for two sets of responses, one in black and the other in red. Choose your color, then dig in for a little self-exploration: Each chapter will lead to some enlightening—and saucy!—discussions along the way.

CHAPTER 1

The Big Ones

What's your big-picture view on love and relationships? Get to know where you both stand on matters philosophical (does true love exist?) and practical (what qualities do I value in a relationship?). Not only will you learn about your partner, you might even discover something new about yourself.

The Intangibles

Love is . . .

. . . spiritual ☐ ☐

. . . emotional ☐ ☐

. . . chemical ☐ ☐

Love means. . .

. . . being willing to ☐ ☐
change for someone

. . . understanding that ☐ ☐
you can't change
your partner

Relationships . . .

. . . shouldn't be hard if you're truly in love ☐ ☐

. . . take a lot of work ☐ ☐

Each person on earth has only one true love.

☐ true ☐ false | ☐ true ☐ false

I believe in fate and destiny.

☐ true ☐ false | ☐ true ☐ false

It is possible to be in love with more than one person at the same time.

☐ true ☐ false | ☐ true ☐ false

In any relationship, there is always one person who is more in love.

☐ true ☐ false | ☐ true ☐ false

If I had to choose between the two, I'd rather be:

☐ loved but not in love ☐ in love, but not loved
☐ loved but not in love ☐ in love, but not loved

Love conquers all.

☐ absolutely ☐ don't be ridiculous
☐ absolutely ☐ don't be ridiculous

Having sex and making love are two different things.
□ true □ false | □ true □ false

It's possible to gradually grow attracted to
a mate you're not attracted to.

□ true □ false | □ true □ false

Good relationships are just about aligning your
quirks and flaws with someone else's.

□ true □ false | □ true □ false

It's important to be friends with my mate.

□ true □ false | □ true □ false

If I had to choose one, I'd pick:

□ lifelong love   □ lifelong financial security
□ lifelong love   □ lifelong financial security

Sonnet 116:

Let me not to the marriage of true minds

William Shakespeare

Let me not to the marriage of true minds
Admit impediments. Love is not love
Which alters when it alteration finds,
Or bends with the remover to remove.
O no! it is an ever-fixed mark
That looks on tempests and is never shaken;
It is the star to every wand'ring bark,
Whose worth's unknown, although his height be
taken.
Love's not Time's fool, though rosy lips and cheeks
Within his bending sickle's compass come;
Love alters not with his brief hours and weeks,
But bears it out even to the edge of doom.
If this be error and upon me prov'd,
I never writ, nor no man ever lov'd.

I'd be willing to sacrifice anything
for someone I loved.

☐ yes ☐ no | ☐ yes ☐ no

I expect someone who loves me to be
willing to sacrifice anything.

☐ yes ☐ no | ☐ yes ☐ no

When you meet the person you're going to
spend the rest of your life with, you just know.

☐ true ☐ false | ☐ true ☐ false

Falling in love is dependent upon:

☐ fate ☐ chance | ☐ fate ☐ chance

Confessing your darkest secrets and fears
with your partner will only bring you closer.

☐ true ☐ false | ☐ true ☐ false

To me, the most taboo sex act is:

_____

_____

_____

_____

The worst crime in the world is:

_____

_____

_____

_____

The best thing you could possibly do for
someone else is:

_____

_____

_____

_____

MY T♥P QUALITIES
IN A PARTNER

Here's how I'd rate the qualities I expect from a partner on a scale from 1 to 10, where 1 is no big deal and 10 is very important.

sense of humor

1 2 3 4 5 6 7 8 9 10

1 2 3 4 5 6 7 8 9 10

religiosity

1 2 3 4 5 6 7 8 9 10

1 2 3 4 5 6 7 8 9 10

libido

1 2 3 4 5 6 7 8 9 10

1 2 3 4 5 6 7 8 9 10

political leanings

1 2 3 4 5 6 7 8 9 10

1 2 3 4 5 6 7 8 9 10

affection

1 2 3 4 5 6 7 8 9 10

1 2 3 4 5 6 7 8 9 10

honesty

1 2 3 4 5 6 7 8 9 10

1 2 3 4 5 6 7 8 9 10

empathy

1 2 3 4 5 6 7 8 9 10

1 2 3 4 5 6 7 8 9 10

communication

1 2 3 4 5 6 7 8 9 10

1 2 3 4 5 6 7 8 9 10

passion

1 2 3 4 5 6 7 8 9 10

1 2 3 4 5 6 7 8 9 10

patience

1 2 3 4 5 6 7 8 9 10

1 2 3 4 5 6 7 8 9 10

ability to listen

1 2 3 4 5 6 7 8 9 10

1 2 3 4 5 6 7 8 9 10

physical attractiveness

1 2 3 4 5 6 7 8 9 10

1 2 3 4 5 6 7 8 9 10

ambition

1 2 3 4 5 6 7 8 9 10

1 2 3 4 5 6 7 8 9 10

cooking ability

1 2 3 4 5 6 7 8 9 10

1 2 3 4 5 6 7 8 9 10

self-discipline

1 2 3 4 5 6 7 8 9 10

1 2 3 4 5 6 7 8 9 10

taste in music and art

1 2 3 4 5 6 7 8 9 10

1 2 3 4 5 6 7 8 9 10

optimism

1 2 3 4 5 6 7 8 9 10

1 2 3 4 5 6 7 8 9 10

parent potential

1 2 3 4 5 6 7 8 9 10

1 2 3 4 5 6 7 8 9 10

dependability

1 2 3 4 5 6 7 8 9 10

1 2 3 4 5 6 7 8 9 10

open-mindedness

1 2 3 4 5 6 7 8 9 10

1 2 3 4 5 6 7 8 9 10

The Tangibles

I'd rather . . .

be with the wrong person than be alone   ☐   ☐

be alone than with the wrong person   ☐   ☐

I want to get married someday.

☐ true ☐ false | ☐ true ☐ false

I want to get married in the next five years.

☐ true ☐ false | ☐ true ☐ false

I want to get married in the next two years.

☐ true ☐ false | ☐ true ☐ false

I'm really only interested in a relationship that has marriage potential.

☐ true ☐ false | ☐ true ☐ false

It's okay to have sex before marriage.

☐ true ☐ false | ☐ true ☐ false

Sex is . . .

the most important thing ☐ ☐

important ☐ ☐

not important ☐ ☐

Sex without love is . . .

good clean fun ☐ ☐

naughty dirty fun ☐ ☐

wrong ☐ ☐

a workout ☐ ☐

not as much fun as sex with love ☐ ☐

Pornography is . . .

not something I can tolerate, ever ☐ ☐

fine, as long as you don't watch
or look at it while I'm around ☐ ☐

fine, as long as it's something
we're enjoying together ☐ ☐

really beginning to take up a
lot of space in my hard drive ☐ ☐

The thing I like most about the idea of settling
down with someone is:

_____

_____

_____

_____

My biggest fear about getting into a committed
relationship is:

_____

_____

_____

_____

The most important qualities in a committed
relationship are:

_____

_____

_____

_____

If we accidentally got pregnant and we weren't married, I'd:

_____

_____

_____

_____

If I wanted kids and discovered I couldn't have them, I'd:

_____

_____

_____

_____

If I wanted kids and discovered my mate couldn't have them, I'd:

_____

_____

_____

_____

CHAPTER 2

Dealbreakers

All couples face disagreement and conflict, but it's important to know your limits (and your partner's!) when considering whether you're in it for the long haul. From religion and politics to kids and infidelity, certain major life choices may be negotiable in some relationships but disqualifying in others. Know where you and your partner stand on the following common dealbreakers.

Spirituality

I consider myself:

religious	☐	☐
deeply religious	☐	☐
spiritual, but not religious	☐	☐
agnostic	☐	☐
searching	☐	☐
atheist	☐	☐
not sure	☐	☐

I believe that . . .

we are here to enjoy this world, now	☐	☐
we are here to sacrifice for greater rewards later	☐	☐

Religion . . .

causes more suffering than good	☐	☐
causes more good than suffering	☐	☐

Other faiths are just as valid as mine.

☐ yes ☐ no ☐certain ones yes, certain ones, no

☐ yes ☐ no ☐certain ones yes, certain ones, no

All or most faiths are praying to the same thing that
they call by different names.

☐ true ☐ false | ☐ true ☐ false

I believe that many organized religions could
benefit by gaining more of a sense of humor.

☐ true ☐ false | ☐ true ☐ false

Is it possible to have faith and believe in evolution?

☐ yes ☐ no | ☐ yes ☐ no

People who are religious are clinging to
old superstitions.

☐ true ☐ false | ☐ true ☐ false

I believe that the world is basically a good place.

☐ true ☐ false | ☐ true ☐ false

I attend religious services regularly.

☐ true ☐ false | ☐ true ☐ false

I prefer to start my meals with grace.

☐ true ☐ false | ☐ true ☐ false

I feel better if I start each day with prayer
or meditation.

☐ true ☐ false | ☐ true ☐ false

I believe that proselytizing is a key part of my faith.

☐ true ☐ false | ☐ true ☐ false

I would feel comfortable in a long-term relationship
with someone who would like to convert me
to his or her faith.

☐ true ☐ false | ☐ true ☐ false

I would be able to spend my life with someone
with radically different spiritual views.

☐ yes ☐ no | ☐ yes ☐ no

I could get married to someone of another religion.

absolutely	☐	☐
absolutely not	☐	☐
yes, but my family would be upset	☐	☐
yes, with some reservations	☐	☐
only if they converted	☐	☐
date, yes; marry, no	☐	☐

I am concerned about my partner and I being able to spend eternity together.

☐ yes ☐ no | ☐ yes ☐ no

I am concerned that my partner's faith might come before our relationship.

☐ yes ☐ no | ☐ yes ☐ no

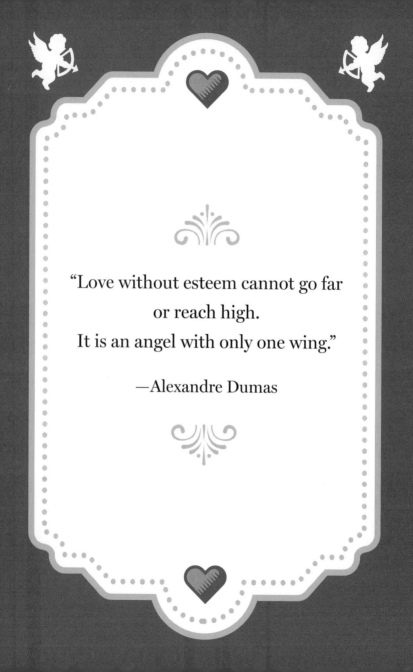

"Love without esteem cannot go far
or reach high.
It is an angel with only one wing."

—Alexandre Dumas

Politics

I consider myself . . .

green	☐	☐
liberal	☐	☐
ultra-liberal	☐	☐
moderate	☐	☐
conservative	☐	☐
neocon	☐	☐
ultra-conservative	☐	☐
libertarian	☐	☐
I take it on an issue-by-issue basis	☐	☐
I don't follow politics	☐	☐

other:

_____

_____

When it comes to the news, I . . .

like to keep informed	☐	☐
just don't have time for it	☐	☐
find it too depressing	☐	☐
am a complete news junkie	☐	☐

To me, the most important political issue right now is . . .

the environment	☐	☐
healthcare	☐	☐
the population explosion	☐	☐
terrorism	☐	☐
poverty	☐	☐
family values	☐	☐
racism	☐	☐
gay rights	☐	☐
the economy	☐	☐
globalization	☐	☐
education	☐	☐

other:

_____

_____

I have . . .

taken part in demonstrations	☐	☐
acted for a political cause	☐	☐
donated to political causes	☐	☐
never done any of those	☐	☐

News Go-Tos

Here are my main sources of news.
(Check all that apply.)

TV:

☐ CNN ☐ CNBC ☐ Fox News ☐ BBC
☐ MSNBC ☐ E! ☐ C-SPAN

☐ CNN ☐ CNBC ☐ Fox News ☐ BBC
☐ MSNBC ☐ E! ☐ C-SPAN

Newspaper:

☐ *New York Times* ☐ *Wall Street Journal*
☐ *Washington Post* ☐ *New York Post* ☐ *Los Angeles Times*

☐ *New York Times* ☐ *Wall Street Journal*
☐ *Washington Post* ☐ *New York Post* ☐ *Los Angeles Times*

Online:

☐ Twitter ☐ Facebook ☐ Breitbart ☐ Huffington Post
☐ The Drudge Report ☐ Townhall ☐ The Daily Beast

☐ Twitter ☐ Facebook ☐ Breitbart ☐ Huffington Post
☐ The Drudge Report ☐ Townhall ☐ The Daily Beast

Magazines:

☐ *Time* ☐ *National Review* ☐ *The Atlantic* ☐ *American
Spectator* ☐ *New Yorker* ☐ *Mother Jones* ☐ *USA Today*

☐ *Time* ☐ *National Review* ☐ *The Atlantic* ☐ *American
Spectator* ☐ *New Yorker* ☐ *Mother Jones* ☐ *USA Today*

I would be able to spend my life with someone who had different political views than mine.

☐ yes ☐ no | ☐ yes ☐ no

I would be able to listen to my partner talk about his or her political views during an entire cocktail party without once rolling my eyes.

☐ yes ☐ no | ☐ yes ☐ no

I would be able to go to sleep at night next to someone who voted differently than I did in the last U.S. presidential election.

☐ yes ☐ no | ☐ yes ☐ no

It's okay if my partner cares much more about politics than I do.

☐ yes ☐ no | ☐ yes ☐ no

It's okay if my partner cares much less about politics than I do.

☐ yes ☐ no | ☐ yes ☐ no

Drugs and Alcohol

My general attitude toward drugs is . . .

the more, the merrier!	☐	☐
occasional use is okay, as long as you don't form any habits	☐	☐
I don't have a problem with experimenting	☐	☐
pot and alcohol are okay, hard drugs are not	☐	☐
alcohol is okay, drugs are not	☐	☐
no drugs, no alcohol, ever	☐	☐

Drinking a cocktail or a beer or two every day is . . .

normal	☐	☐
a bad pattern	☐	☐

Smoking a joint every day is . . .

unacceptable	☐	☐
a little too much	☐	☐
okay in college, but not for real adults	☐	☐
my usual	☐	☐

Hallucinogens are . . .

mind-expanding	☐	☐
harmless	☐	☐
dangerous	☐	☐

When I drink, it's . . .

only once in a while, on social occasions	☐	☐
usually just one or two after work or with dinner	☐	☐
usually several, at parties	☐	☐
usually until I'm out of control	☐	☐
a nonalcoholic beverage	☐	☐

Drinking to the point of throwing up or a hangover is . . .

something I do most weekends	☐	☐
something I did in high school or college	☐	☐
something I don't approve of	☐	☐

Drinking before sex:

relaxes me	☐	☐
I can take it or leave it	☐	☐
shouldn't happen at all	☐	☐
needs to happen every time	☐	☐
is okay some of the time, but I'd worry if it were every time	☐	☐

Smoking pot before sex:

relaxes me	☐	☐
I can take it or leave it	☐	☐
shouldn't happen at all	☐	☐
needs to happen every time	☐	☐
is okay some of the time, but I'd worry if it were every time	☐	☐

I've slept with someone while drunk who I wouldn't
have slept with completely sober.

☐ true ☐ false | ☐ true ☐ false

Knowing that you had slept with someone while
drunk who you wouldn't have slept with completely
sober would make me feel . . .

like I couldn't trust you	☐	☐
not bad—we all screw up sometimes	☐	☐
uncomfortable	☐	☐
a certain kinship with you	☐	☐

I could date someone who doesn't drink at all
or drinks much less than I do.

☐ true ☐ false | ☐ true ☐ false

I could date someone who drinks
quite a bit more than I do.

☐ true ☐ false | ☐ true ☐ false

I could date someone who doesn't do drugs
at all or does much less than I do.

☐ true ☐ false | ☐ true ☐ false

I could date someone who does more drugs than I do.

☐ true ☐ false | ☐ true ☐ false

Past experimentation with drugs is okay.

☐ true ☐ false | ☐ true ☐ false

I could date a recovering drug addict.

☐ true ☐ false | ☐ true ☐ false

I could date a recovering alcoholic.

☐ true ☐ false | ☐ true ☐ false

I am a recovering drug addict or alcoholic.

☐ true ☐ false ☐ I'm thinking about entering a
program

☐ true ☐ false ☐ I'm thinking about entering a
program

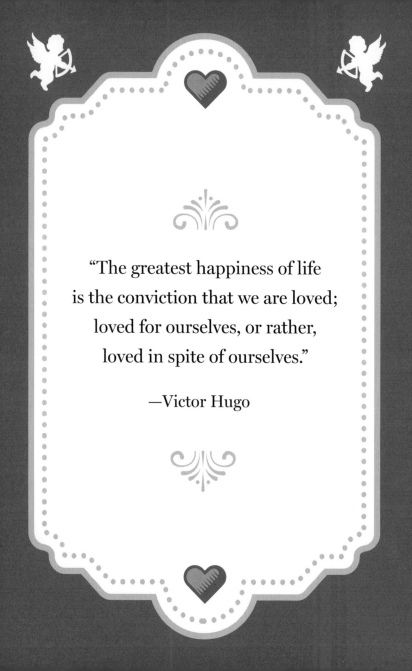

"The greatest happiness of life
is the conviction that we are loved;
loved for ourselves, or rather,
loved in spite of ourselves."

—Victor Hugo

Cheating

I've been cheated on before.

☐ yes ☐ no ☐ no proof, but pretty sure it happened
☐ yes ☐ no ☐ no proof, but pretty sure it happened

I expect our relationship to be exclusive once
we start sleeping together.

☐ yes ☐ no | ☐ yes ☐ no

I expect our relationship to be exclusive once
we've been dating for . . .

six months	☐	☐
three months	☐	☐
a month	☐	☐
one date	☐	☐
it depends	☐	☐

Having sex with someone else is only cheating if we've
had a talk and specifically agreed to be exclusive.

☐ true ☐ false | ☐ true ☐ false

I'd be willing to be a part of an open relationship.

☐ yes ☐ no | ☐ yes ☐ no

Flirting with someone else at a party is . . .

exciting ☐ ☐
harmless ☐ ☐
creepy ☐ ☐
cheating ☐ ☐

Kissing someone else is cheating.

☐ true ☐ false | ☐ true ☐ false

Giving a back massage or foot massage
to someone else is cheating.

☐ true ☐ false | ☐ true ☐ false

Flirting or chatting on platforms like Snapchat
or Facebook is cheating.

☐ true ☐ false | ☐ true ☐ false

If you did cheat, I'd rather . . .

☐ know ☐ not know | ☐ know ☐ not know

I'd be more upset by . . .

a one-night stand, purely for sex ☐ ☐
a longtime close emotional
attachment that never led to sex ☐ ☐

The worst consequence of cheating is:

jealousy	☐	☐
the lack of trust	☐	☐
the risk of STDs	☐	☐
other:		

_____

_____

I'd be able to forgive you if you had a one-night stand.

☐ yes ☐ no ☐ I don't know
☐ yes ☐ no ☐ I don't know

I'd be able to forgive you if you had an affair.

☐ yes ☐ no ☐ I don't know
☐ yes ☐ no ☐ I don't know

If I caught you cheating, I'd expect to have payback sex with someone else.

☐ yes ☐ no ☐ I'd at least let you think I would
☐ yes ☐ no ☐ I'd at least let you think I would

Keeping in touch with ex-girlfriends or
ex-boyfriends is a sign of . . .

an ability to handle
breakups maturely ☐ ☐

an unwillingness to let go
of the past ☐ ☐

It's okay for you to spend the day with an ex.

☐ yes ☐ no ☐ depends on the ex in question

☐ yes ☐ no ☐ depends on the ex in question

If I could choose one ex you'd never spend time with
again, it would be:

_____

_____

It's okay for you to hang out alone with a friend
who's the same gender as I am.

☐ yes ☐ no ┃ ☐ yes ☐ no

It's okay for you to hang out alone with a really hot friend who's the same gender as I am.

☐ yes ☐ no | ☐ yes ☐ no

I'd be okay with you going to see a stripper with your friends.

☐ true ☐ false | ☐ true ☐ false

I'd be okay with you going to see a stripper with me.

☐ true ☐ false | ☐ true ☐ false

Strippers at a bachelor or bachelorette party don't count.

☐ true ☐ false | ☐ true ☐ false

In all honesty, I get jealous when you:

_____

_____

_____

_____

Making a list of five celebrities that each of us gets a free pass to sleep with is . . .

fun ☐ ☐
inexplicable ☐ ☐

And, by the way, here's my list:

1. _____

2. _____

3. _____

4. _____

5. _____

And here's mine:

1. _____

2. _____

3. _____

4. _____

5. _____

Kids

I want kids.

nope	☐	☐
I'm not sure	☐	☐
yes, one	☐	☐
yes, two or three	☐	☐
yes, several	☐	☐

I'm willing to commit to someone who
doesn't want kids.

☐ yes ☐ no | ☐ yes ☐ no

I'm willing to commit to someone who wants kids.

☐ yes ☐ no | ☐ yes ☐ no

I'm willing to commit to someone who isn't sure.

☐ yes ☐ no | ☐ yes ☐ no

I feel like I want or need to start having kids . . .

within ten years	☐	☐
within five years	☐	☐
within two years	☐	☐
seriously, I don't want kids	☐	☐

If we can't get pregnant naturally, let's try:

fertility treatments ☐ ☐

adoption ☐ ☐

fostering ☐ ☐

to forget it ☐ ☐

The baby names we choose should be:

after family members ☐ ☐

traditional ☐ ☐

unique ☐ ☐

let's wing it! ☐ ☐

The gender should be:

a secret until birth ☐ ☐

a secret until the gender
reveal party ☐ ☐

tell me, asap ☐ ☐

After the baby is born, I expect that:

we'll both take parental leave ☐ ☐

only I will take leave ☐ ☐

only you will take leave ☐ ☐

I'll quit my job ☐ ☐

I would . . .

prefer to adopt than conceive naturally	☐	☐
consider adoption	☐	☐
not be willing to adopt	☐	☐

I'd be willing to take in a foster child.

☐ yes ☐ no │ ☐ yes ☐ no

I'd be willing to foster or adopt an older child.

☐ yes ☐ no │ ☐ yes ☐ no

I'd be willing to adopt a child of another race.

☐ yes ☐ no │ ☐ yes ☐ no

I would tell my child their adoption story
when it's age appropriate.

☐ yes ☐ no │ ☐ yes ☐ no

I'd be willing to participate in an open or semi-open
adoption, where there is some contact with the
biological family.

☐ yes ☐ no │ ☐ yes ☐ no

Five baby name no-nos for me are:

_____   _____

_____   _____

_____   _____

_____   _____

_____   _____

Five baby name faves are:

_____   _____

_____   _____

_____   _____

_____   _____

_____   _____

I'm willing to commit to someone who already has kids.

☐ yes ☐ no | ☐ yes ☐ no

I'm willing to commit to someone who already has kids and wants more with me.

☐ yes ☐ no | ☐ yes ☐ no

I'm willing to commit to someone who already has kids and doesn't want any more.

☐ yes ☐ no | ☐ yes ☐ no

Assuming we both have kids, I'd expect to spend holidays . . .

all together	☐	☐
with one side of the family or the other	☐	☐
just as a couple	☐	☐
we'll play it by ear each time	☐	☐

If I have to err on one side or the other, I believe it's best to give kids a little too much . . .

freedom ☐ ☐

discipline ☐ ☐

I expect to educate my kids . . .

by home-school ☐ ☐

at a private school ☐ ☐

at a public school ☐ ☐

I believe it's more important to . . .

focus on making us work as
a couple ☐ ☐

focus on the kids ☐ ☐

Divorce is not an option if kids are involved.

☐ true ☐ false ┃ ☐ true ☐ false

Kids should only get an allowance if they
earn it through chores.

☐ yes ☐ no ┃ ☐ yes ☐ no

My priority in raising kids will be to:

emphasize education and career	☐	☐
nurture their compassion for others	☐	☐
instill a connection to their faith	☐	☐
build friendships with them	☐	☐
ensure they start a family	☐	☐

I think it's okay for kids to start dating at age:

_____   _____

I think the best way to raise good kids is to:

_____

_____

_____

_____

_____

_____

Dealbreaker Rankings (1–20)

Here are my relationship dealbreakers ranked from
1 (simply annoying) to 20 (disqualifying).

Smoking   ____   ____
Alcohol   ____   ____
Cheating in the past   ____   ____
Children from past relationship   ____   ____
Religion   ____   ____
Race   ____   ____
STDs   ____   ____
Infertility   ____   ____
Sexual prowess   ____   ____
Poor hygiene   ____   ____
Anger issues   ____   ____
Musical taste   ____   ____
Punctuality   ____   ____
Poor manners   ____   ____
Low self-esteem   ____   ____
Egotism   ____   ____
Financial ineptitude   ____   ____
Snoring   ____   ____
Lack of goals/ambition   ____   ____
Stinginess   ____   ____

My Personal Dealbreakers

Clothing is a dealbreaker for me.

☐ yes ☐ no ┃ ☐ yes ☐ no

Intelligence is a dealbreaker for me.

☐ yes ☐ no ┃ ☐ yes ☐ no

Musical taste is a dealbreaker for me.

☐ yes ☐ no ┃ ☐ yes ☐ no

Sense of humor is a dealbreaker for me

☐ yes ☐ no ┃ ☐ yes ☐ no

Income is a dealbreaker for me.

☐ yes ☐ no ┃ ☐ yes ☐ no

Gift-giving is a dealbreaker for me.

☐ yes ☐ no ┃ ☐ yes ☐ no

A criminal record is a dealbreaker for me.

☐ yes ☐ no | ☐ yes ☐ no

Education is a dealbreaker for me.

☐ yes ☐ no | ☐ yes ☐ no

Grammar is a dealbreaker for me.

☐ yes ☐ no | ☐ yes ☐ no

Being physically active is a dealbreaker for me.

☐ yes ☐ no | ☐ yes ☐ no

Division of household chores is a dealbreaker for me.

☐ yes ☐ no | ☐ yes ☐ no

Loving my home sports team is a dealbreaker for me.

☐ yes ☐ no | ☐ yes ☐ no

Veganism/vegetarianism is a dealbreaker for me.

☐ yes ☐ no | ☐ yes ☐ no

Constant internet or smart phone use
is a dealbreaker for me.

☐ yes ☐ no | ☐ yes ☐ no

An aversion to pets is a dealbreaker for me.

☐ yes ☐ no | ☐ yes ☐ no

An allergy to pets is a dealbreaker for me.

☐ yes ☐ no | ☐ yes ☐ no

Height is a dealbreaker for me.

☐ yes ☐ no | ☐ yes ☐ no

Hair/baldness is a dealbreaker for me.

☐ yes ☐ no | ☐ yes ☐ no

Personal hygiene is a dealbreaker for me

☐ yes ☐ no ☐ we should talk about that
☐ yes ☐ no ☐ we should talk about that

Video games are a dealbreaker for me.

☐ yes ☐ no | ☐ yes ☐ no

Excessive TV watching is a dealbreaker for me.

☐ yes ☐ no | ☐ yes ☐ no

Gaining or losing a lot of weight would be
a dealbreaker for me.

☐ yes ☐ no | ☐ yes ☐ no

The way someone laughs or smiles is a
dealbreaker for me.

☐ yes ☐ no | ☐ yes ☐ no

Your friends may be a dealbreaker for me.

☐ yes ☐ no | ☐ yes ☐ no

I think your parents may be a dealbreaker for me.

☐ no ☐ we should talk | ☐ no ☐ we should talk

Smoking is a dealbreaker for me.

☐ yes ☐ no | ☐ yes ☐ no

A past marriage is a dealbreaker for me.

☐ yes ☐ no | ☐ yes ☐ no

Sex before marriage is a dealbreaker for me.

☐ yes ☐ no | ☐ yes ☐ no

Oral sex is a dealbreaker for me.

☐ yes ☐ no | ☐ yes ☐ no

The number of sex partners you've had may be a dealbreaker for me.

☐ yes ☐ no | ☐ yes ☐ no

A past encounter with a prostitute is a dealbreaker for me.

☐ yes ☐ no | ☐ yes ☐ no

Multiple past encounters with prostitutes would be a dealbreaker for me.

☐ yes ☐ no | ☐ yes ☐ no

Quality of sex is a dealbreaker for me.

☐ yes ☐ no ☐ we should talk about that
☐ yes ☐ no ☐ we should talk about that

Frequency of sex is a dealbreaker for me.

☐ yes ☐ no ☐ we should talk about that
☐ yes ☐ no ☐ we should talk about that

No sex at all would be a dealbreaker for me.

☐ yes ☐ no ☐ we should talk about that
☐ yes ☐ no ☐ we should talk about that

Another possible dealbreaker that you and I should talk about is:

_____

_____

_____

_____

I Am Not Yours

Sara Teasdale

I am not yours, not lost in you,
Not lost, although I long to be
Lost as a candle lit at noon,
Lost as a snowflake in the sea.

You love me, and I find you still
A spirit beautiful and bright,
Yet I am I, who long to be
Lost as a light is lost in light.

Oh plunge me deep in love—put out
My senses, leave me deaf and blind,
Swept by the tempest of your love,
A taper in a rushing wind.

CHAPTER 3

Our
Relationship

Time for some real talk: How satisfied are you both inside and outside the bedroom? (And what can you do to spice things up?) Which of your partner's habits and quirks do you love, and which do you only tolerate? Coming clean on these intimate topics is not for the bashful, but it'll do wonders for your relationship—from the routine of the day-to-day to the excitement between the sheets.

My Satisfaction

I could use a little more . . .

romance	☐	☐
conversation	☐	☐
help around the house	☐	☐
passion	☐	☐
friendship	☐	☐

If had to choose one, I'd choose . . .

more time together	☐	☐
more space	☐	☐

My general interest in sex is . . .

high	☐	☐
average	☐	☐
low	☐	☐

I'd be more interested in sex if you . . .

_____

_____

_____

_____

My favorite part of sex is . . .

_____

_____

_____

_____

In bed, I'd love you to pay more attention to . . .

_____

_____

_____

_____

I'd love more . . .

cuddling	☐	☐
kissing/making out	☐	☐
quickies	☐	☐
sex in general	☐	☐

I prefer sex to be . . .

gentle	☐	☐
rough	☐	☐
it depends on my mood	☐	☐

I prefer sex . . .

in the morning	☐	☐
at night	☐	☐
in the afternoon	☐	☐

My favorite way to kiss is . . .

no tongue	☐	☐
light tongue	☐	☐
deep kissing with plenty of tongue	☐	☐

The best kiss you ever gave me was:

_____

_____

_____

_____

My favorite time you and I had sex was:

_____

_____

_____

_____

Dirty talk is . . .

hot	☐	☐
gross	☐	☐
silly	☐	☐
essential	☐	☐

I'd like our foreplay to be . . .

longer	☐	☐
shorter	☐	☐

I enjoy lingerie.

true	☐	☐
false	☐	☐

Sex outdoors is . . .

filthy (bad)	☐	☐
filthy (good)	☐	☐

Sex in a car is . . .

exciting	☐	☐
uncomfortable	☐	☐

I'd like . . .

to initiate sex more often	☐	☐
for you to initiate sex more often	☐	☐

The thing I have the most difficulty with in bed is:

_____

_____

_____

_____

You can help me with that by:

_____

_____

_____

_____

I Loved You First

Christina Rossetti

I loved you first: but afterwards your love,
Outsoaring mine, sang such a loftier song
As drowned the friendly cooings of my dove.
Which owes the other most? My love was long,
And yours one moment seemed to wax more strong;
I loved and guessed at you, you construed me
And loved me for what might or might not be—
Nay, weights and measures do us both a wrong.
For verily love knows not "mine" or "thine";
With separate "I" and "thou" free love has done,
For one is both and both are one in love:
Rich love knows nought of "thine that is not mine";
Both have the strength and both the length thereof,
Both of us, of the love which makes us one.

Rating Our Relati♥nship

On a scale of 1 to 10, here's how I'd rate the following qualities in our relationship.

Transparency	____	____
Kindness	____	____
Loyalty	____	____
Forgiveness	____	____
Selflessness	____	____
Communication	____	____
Passion	____	____
Growth	____	____
Knowledge of each other	____	____
Understanding	____	____
Faith in each other	____	____
Joy	____	____
Consistency	____	____
Humility	____	____
Vulnerability	____	____

We should really work on:

_____

_____

My Partner (That's You . . .)

I'm most attracted to you when you are:

talking	☐	☐
sleeping	☐	☐
working out	☐	☐
playing a sport	☐	☐
performing	☐	☐
cooking	☐	☐
dancing	☐	☐
other:		

_____

When I look at you, I feel:

lucky	☐	☐
proud	☐	☐
turned on	☐	☐
other:		

My favorite thing about you is:

your body	☐	☐
your looks	☐	☐
your intelligence	☐	☐
your sense of humor	☐	☐
your talent	☐	☐
your ambition	☐	☐
your values	☐	☐
your stability	☐	☐
your danger	☐	☐
other:		

_____

_____

My feelings for you are:

warm and cozy	☐	☐
hot like fire	☐	☐
tender and caring	☐	☐
respectful and admiring	☐	☐
other:		

_____

_____

The thing I first noticed about you was:

_____

_____

_____

_____

The thing that first attracted me to you was:

_____

_____

_____

_____

At first I didn't like it, but now I love your:

_____

_____

_____

_____

The proudest I've ever been of you was:

_____

_____

_____

_____

The time I felt most taken care of by you was:

_____

_____

_____

_____

I feel safest with you when:

_____

_____

_____

_____

My favorite meal you make is:

_____

_____

_____

_____

My favorite outfit of yours is:

_____

_____

_____

_____

My least favorite article of your clothing is:

_____

_____

_____

_____

You don't know it, but I love it when you:

_____

_____

_____

_____

I love watching you:

_____

_____

_____

_____

The thing I've learned about you that surprised me the most is:

_____

_____

_____

_____

You're at your best when you:

_____

_____

_____

You're funniest when you:

_____

_____

_____

My favorite little habit of yours is:

_____

_____

_____

_____

Three things about you that I love, but I'm not sure you know about are:

1. _____

2. _____

3. _____

1. _____

2. _____

3. _____

I love it when I catch you:

talking to yourself	☐	☐
playing air guitar	☐	☐
singing in the shower	☐	☐
playing with a pet	☐	☐
daydreaming	☐	☐
other:		

_____

_____

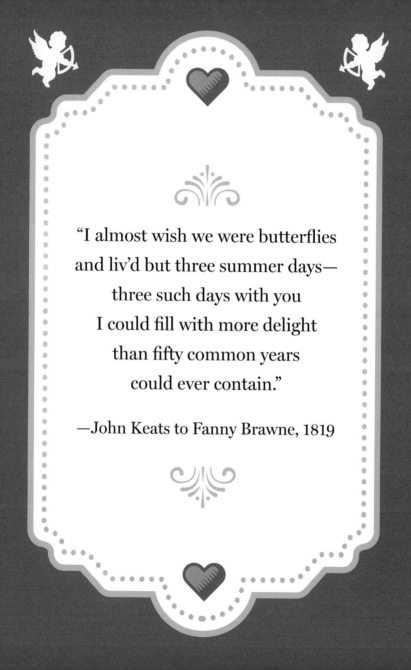

"I almost wish we were butterflies
and liv'd but three summer days—
three such days with you
I could fill with more delight
than fifty common years
could ever contain."

—John Keats to Fanny Brawne, 1819

The thing I'd most like to know about you is:

_____

_____

_____

_____

If money were no object, I'd give you:

_____

_____

_____

_____

If I could replace or update one of your possessions,
it would be:

_____

_____

_____

_____

My favorite thing you do in the morning is:

_____

_____

My least favorite thing you do in the morning is:

_____

_____

My favorite thing you do before bed is:

_____

_____

My least favorite thing you do before bed is:

_____

_____

My favorite part of your body is your:

_____

_____

_____

_____

The body part that you don't like but I secretly love
is your:

_____

_____

_____

_____

I get a little crush on you all over again when you:

_____

_____

_____

_____

You're physically my type because . . .

_____

_____

_____

_____

Your personality fits my type because . . .

_____

_____

_____

_____

You're different from anyone else I've dated because . . .

_____

_____

_____

_____

When we're alone, I notice that you:

_____

_____

_____

_____

When we're in public, I love it when you:

_____

_____

_____

_____

When we're in public, I dislike it when you:

_____

_____

_____

_____

The weirdest dream I've ever had about you is:

_____

_____

_____

_____

I think it means:

_____

_____

_____

_____

I'm worried that I don't do this well enough for you:

_____

_____

_____

_____

I feel most confident around you when:

_____

_____

My favorite thing to do together is:

_____

_____

The friend of yours I most admire:

_____

_____

When you're with your friends, I notice that you:

_____

_____

_____

_____

A little habit you have that turns me off is:

_____

_____

_____

_____

You think I love it, but I really just tolerate it:

_____

_____

_____

_____

The closest you've come to losing me was when you:

_____

_____

_____

_____

I wish you knew how great you are at:

_____

_____

_____

_____

I wish you would ask me more about:

_____

_____

_____

_____

I wish you would talk more about:

_____

_____

_____

_____

I wish I could see more of your . . .

masculine side	☐	☐
feminine side	☐	☐

Seeing you cry makes me feel . . .

closer to you	☐	☐
uncomfortable	☐	☐
less respect for you	☐	☐
eager to comfort you	☐	☐

When you're jealous, it makes me feel . . .

attractive and taken care of	☐	☐
like you don't trust me	☐	☐

When you're angry, it makes me . . .

want to calm you down	☐	☐
want to leave	☐	☐
afraid	☐	☐
annoyed	☐	☐
other:		

_____

_____

The member of your family I feel most comfortable with:

_____

_____

The member of your family I think you're most like:

_____

_____

The member of your family I'd most like to improve my relationship with:

_____

_____

. . . And here's how you can help with that:

_____

_____

Our Milest♥nes

Here's a list of our firsts and bests as a couple:

Where we met

_____   _____

Our first kiss

_____   _____

Our best date

_____   _____

Our song

_____   _____

Our restaurant

_____   _____

Our emojis

_____   _____

The first movie we saw together

_____   _____

Our first binge-watch

_____   _____

The first concert we went to

_____   _____

The first time you cooked for me (and vice-versa)

_____   _____

Our first sleepover

_____   _____

The first time we met each other's friends

_____   _____

The first time we met each other's families

_____   _____

The first time we said "I love you"

_____   _____

Our first fight

_____   _____

Our first joint purchase

_____   _____

Our first trip

_____   _____

Our first anniversary celebration

_____   _____

My Wishes

The one thing I'd most like you to try in bed is:

_____

_____

_____

_____

The place I'd most like to try having sex is:

_____

_____

_____

_____

Food and sex . . .

don't mix   ☐   ☐

double your pleasure   ☐   ☐

The idea of trying phone sex is . . .

appealing	☐	☐
not appealing	☐	☐
out of the question	☐	☐
routine	☐	☐

The idea of hearing someone else having sex is . . .

appealing	☐	☐
not appealing	☐	☐
out of the question	☐	☐
routine	☐	☐

The idea of being overheard while we have sex is . . .

appealing	☐	☐
not appealing	☐	☐
out of the question	☐	☐
routine	☐	☐

The idea of seeing someone else have sex is . . .

appealing	☐	☐
not appealing	☐	☐
out of the question	☐	☐
routine	☐	☐

The idea of being watched while we have sex is . . .

appealing	☐	☐
not appealing	☐	☐
out of the question	☐	☐
routine	☐	☐

The idea of photographing or videotaping ourselves is . . .

appealing	☐	☐
not appealing	☐	☐
out of the question	☐	☐
routine	☐	☐

The idea of trying cybersex is . . .

appealing	☐	☐
not appealing	☐	☐
out of the question	☐	☐
routine	☐	☐

The idea of having sex on an airplane is . . .

appealing	☐	☐
not appealing	☐	☐
out of the question	☐	☐
routine	☐	☐
I'm a Mile-High Club frequent flier	☐	☐

The idea of experimenting with gender roles is . . .

appealing	☐	☐
not appealing	☐	☐
out of the question	☐	☐
routine	☐	☐

The idea of role playing is . . .

appealing	☐	☐
not appealing	☐	☐
out of the question	☐	☐
routine	☐	☐

. . . And the most interesting roles for me would involve:

military uniforms	☐	☐
a French maid's outfit	☐	☐
a stripper pole	☐	☐
pizza delivery	☐	☐
jungle loincloths	☐	☐
doctors or nurses	☐	☐
the old West	☐	☐
the middle ages	☐	☐
let's try em all!	☐	☐
other:		

_____

_____

Compatibility Potp♥urri

If I had to pick just one, I'd take:

early morning	☐	☐
late night	☐	☐
Jimmy Fallon	☐	☐
Trevor Noah	☐	☐
casino	☐	☐
bowling alley	☐	☐
Facebook	☐	☐
Instagram	☐	☐
thriller	☐	☐
comedy	☐	☐
Jeopardy	☐	☐
Wheel of Fortune	☐	☐
concert tickets	☐	☐
baseball tickets	☐	☐

CHAPTER 4

My Foundation

You can learn plenty about your partner by way of their expectations, desires, likes, and dislikes, but you'll gain an even deeper understanding of the person they are today by learning about their upbringing. Parents, family, friends, and all the milestones of childhood and adolescence can shape our views on relationships and the world. So get ready to dig deep and uncover their origin story as well as your own.

My Parents

My parents . . .

stayed married, happily	☐	☐
stayed married, unhappily	☐	☐
divorced, amicably	☐	☐
divorced, bitterly	☐	☐

The thing I liked most about my parents'
(or parent and stepparent's) relationship is:

_____

_____

_____

One thing in my parents' relationship that I would
never bring to my relationship is:

_____

_____

_____

_____

My favorite thing to do with my dad when I was little was:

_____

_____

My favorite thing to do with my mom when I was little was:

_____

_____

My favorite thing to do with my dad now is:

_____

_____

My favorite thing to do with my mom now is:

_____

_____

When my parents were angry with me,
they would:

discuss it quietly	☐	☐
yell	☐	☐
hit	☐	☐
give me a time-out	☐	☐
give me the silent treatment	☐	☐
other:		

_____

_____

When my parents were angry with each other,
they would:

hide it	☐	☐
discuss it in normal speaking voices	☐	☐
shout at each other	☐	☐
fight physically	☐	☐
other:		

_____

_____

My parents showed affection to each other
in front of me by:

saying nice things to each other	☐	☐
holding hands or hugging	☐	☐
kissing	☐	☐
wrestling	☐	☐
my parents didn't show physical affection to each other	☐	☐

other:

_____

_____

My parents showed physical affection to me by:

hugging or kissing me in private	☐	☐
hugging me in public	☐	☐
playful wrestling or hair-tousling	☐	☐
my parents didn't show physical affection to me	☐	☐

other:

_____

_____

My mother told me she loved me:

daily	☐	☐
often	☐	☐
seldom	☐	☐
never	☐	☐

My father told me he loved me:

daily	☐	☐
often	☐	☐
seldom	☐	☐
never	☐	☐

My parents showed an interest in my day-to-day life:

always	☐	☐
often	☐	☐
seldom	☐	☐
never	☐	☐

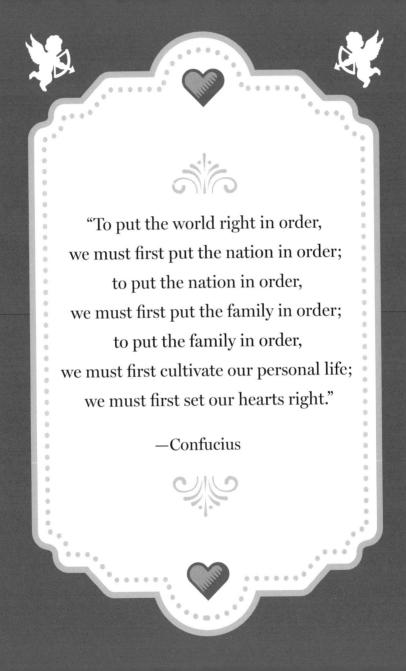

"To put the world right in order,
we must first put the nation in order;
to put the nation in order,
we must first put the family in order;
to put the family in order,
we must first cultivate our personal life;
we must first set our hearts right."

—Confucius

The best thing my mom did while raising me was:

_____

_____

The best thing my dad did while raising me was:

_____

_____

One thing I wish my parents had done for me is:

_____

_____

One thing my parents did that I'll never do to my kids was:

_____

_____

When I started dating, my parents were:

overprotective	☐	☐
too lenient	☐	☐
just about right	☐	☐

My parents taught me about sex . . .

early on	☐	☐
way too late	☐	☐
at about the right time	☐	☐

My parents taught me that sex is . . .

fun	☐	☐
good and pleasurable	☐	☐
dirty or bad	☐	☐
only for married people	☐	☐
only for procreation	☐	☐

When my parents discussed love and sex with me, they were . . .

frank and comfortable	☐	☐
uncomfortable	☐	☐
unwilling to talk	☐	☐
they never discussed love and sex with me	☐	☐

I think that my parents . . .

mostly approve of the way I handle my relationships	☐	☐
mostly disapprove of the way I handle my relationships	☐	☐

. . . And that's:

a good thing	☐	☐
a bad thing	☐	☐
not something I care about	☐	☐

Here's how I think my parents have shaped my attitudes toward relationships:

_____

_____

My Childhood

When I was a child, I loved to:

play sports	☐	☐
play board games	☐	☐
make up stories	☐	☐
play with dolls	☐	☐
go exploring	☐	☐
read	☐	☐

well, actually what I most liked was to:

_____

_____

The grandparent I was closest to:

_____

_____

Because:

_____

_____

The subject in school I was best at:

_____

_____

The subject in school I was worst at:

_____

_____

My favorite teacher was:

_____

_____

The coolest thing I could draw was:

_____

_____

My favorite hobby was

_____

_____

I am . . .

an only child	☐	☐
one of two kids	☐	☐
one of many	☐	☐

If I was not an only child, I was . . .

an older sibling	☐	☐
a younger sibling	☐	☐
a middle sibling	☐	☐
a stepsibling or half-sibling	☐	☐

I always wished I'd had . . .

an older brother	☐	☐
a younger brother	☐	☐
an older sister	☐	☐
a younger sister	☐	☐
more siblings in general	☐	☐
more space to myself	☐	☐
none of these—I was perfectly happy	☐	☐

Okay, I'll admit it . . .

as an only child, I still have trouble sharing	☐	☐
as an older sibling, I still like to boss people around	☐	☐
as a younger sibling, I'm still used to being taken care of	☐	☐
as a middle sibling, I still feel like I have to fight for attention	☐	☐

none of those, but I do have to admit that:

_____

_____

One adult who encouraged me was:

_____

_____

One adult who discouraged me was:

_____

_____

The best thing an adult ever said to me when
I was a kid:

_____

_____

If I could erase one thing an adult said to me when I
was a kid, it would be:

_____

_____

When I was a kid, I was afraid of:

_____

_____

My favorite fairy tale or bedtime story was:

_____

_____

This made me feel safe because:

_____

_____

When I was a kid, my favorite married or
long-term couple was:

_____

_____

My favorite aunt or uncle was:

_____

_____

My first pet's name:

_____

_____

My favorite pet:

_____

_____

My best friend as a child:

_____

_____

When I was a kid, I loved to pretend to be:

_____

_____

When I was a kid, I was sure I'd grow up to be:

_____

_____

When I was a kid, I thought I'd marry:

_____

_____

My biggest celebrity crush as an adolescent was:

_____

_____

What I liked most about my crush was:

_____

_____

Here's how you remind me of my old crush:

_____

_____

What's embarrassing now about my crush:

_____

_____

My first childhood boyfriend or girlfriend was:

_____

_____

What I liked about him or her was:

_____

_____

My first real boyfriend or girlfriend was:

_____

_____

What I liked about him or her was:

_____

_____

My first real heartbreak was:

_____

_____

I practiced getting married as a kid.

□ true □ false | □ true □ false

I fantasized about my wedding. . .

constantly	□	□
sometimes	□	□
once or twice	□	□
never thought about it	□	□

I played doctor as a kid.

yes, with friends of the same sex	□	□
yes, with friends of the opposite sex	□	□
yes, with friends of both sexes	□	□
I never played doctor	□	□

I played spin the bottle, post office, or other kissing games . . .

as a kid	□	□
in high school	□	□
in college	□	□
as an adult	□	□
never	□	□

In high school I was:

a nerd	☐	☐
a mean girl	☐	☐
a jock	☐	☐
a cheerleader	☐	☐
a class representative	☐	☐
a stoner	☐	☐
a punk	☐	☐
a goth	☐	☐
a prep	☐	☐
an emo kid	☐	☐
a ghost	☐	☐

other:

_____

_____

_____

_____

Lifelines

Who would you go to for help in the following situations? Check all that apply.

Conflict at work:

family ☐ friend ☐ partner ☐ therapist ☐ religious leader ☐
family ☐ friend ☐ partner ☐ therapist ☐ religious leader ☐

Painful breakup or relationship drama:

family ☐ friend ☐ therapist ☐ an ex ☐ religious leader ☐
family ☐ friend ☐ therapist ☐ an ex ☐ religious leader ☐

Managing depression:

family ☐ friend ☐ partner ☐ therapist ☐ religious leader ☐
family ☐ friend ☐ partner ☐ therapist ☐ religious leader ☐

Fertility problems:

family ☐ friend ☐ partner ☐ therapist ☐ religious leader ☐
family ☐ friend ☐ partner ☐ therapist ☐ religious leader ☐

Parenting issues or discipline problems with kids:

family ☐ friend ☐ partner ☐ therapist ☐ religious leader ☐
family ☐ friend ☐ partner ☐ therapist ☐ religious leader ☐

Medical issues:

family ☐ friend ☐ partner ☐ therapist ☐ religious leader ☐
family ☐ friend ☐ partner ☐ therapist ☐ religious leader ☐

Financial troubles:

family ☐ friend ☐ partner ☐ therapist ☐ religious leader ☐
family ☐ friend ☐ partner ☐ therapist ☐ religious leader ☐

Addictions:

family ☐ friend ☐ partner ☐ therapist ☐ religious leader ☐
family ☐ friend ☐ partner ☐ therapist ☐ religious leader ☐

Sexual dissatisfaction:

family ☐ friend ☐ partner ☐ therapist ☐ religious leader ☐
family ☐ friend ☐ partner ☐ therapist ☐ religious leader ☐

Grief over the loss of a loved one:

family ☐ friend ☐ partner ☐ therapist ☐ religious leader ☐
family ☐ friend ☐ partner ☐ therapist ☐ religious leader ☐

Low self-esteem:

family ☐ friend ☐ partner ☐ therapist ☐ religious leader ☐
family ☐ friend ☐ partner ☐ therapist ☐ religious leader ☐

Uncertainty about sexual and/or gender identity:

family ☐ friend ☐ partner ☐ therapist ☐ religious leader ☐
family ☐ friend ☐ partner ☐ therapist ☐ religious leader ☐

CHAPTER 5

My Past

Opening up about past relationships—both the good and the bad—can be daunting. But remember that you both have unique stories and wisdoms to bring to your current relationship. Sharing these experiences with a partner, however embarrassing it might feel, will offer insight into who you are now and what you've learned as those old scars have healed.

My Baggage

Three things I wish I'd done differently in my last relationship:

1. _____

_____

2. _____

_____

3. _____

_____

1. _____

_____

2. _____

_____

3. _____

_____

Three things I wish my last partner had done differently:

1. _____

_____

2. _____

_____

3. _____

_____

1. _____

_____

2. _____

_____

3. _____

_____

My most difficult challenge in life:

_____

_____

_____

_____

The worst trouble I've gotten into:

_____

_____

_____

_____

My biggest failure:

_____

_____

_____

_____

I think I should have loved you presently (Sonnet IX)

Edna St. Vincent Millay

I think I should have loved you presently,
And given in earnest words I flung in jest;
And lifted honest eyes for you to see,
And caught your hand against my cheek and breast;
And all my pretty follies flung aside
That won you to me, and beneath your gaze,
Naked of reticence and shorn of pride,
Spread like a chart my little wicked ways.
I, that had been to you, had you remained,
But one more waking from a recurrent dream,
Cherish no less the certain stakes I gained,
And walk your memory's halls, austere, supreme,
A ghost in marble of a girl you knew
Who would have loved you in a day or two.

Looking back, I regret more . . .

things I've done	☐	☐
things I haven't done	☐	☐

I've cheated on an ex and been caught.

☐ true ☐ false | ☐ true ☐ false

I've cheated on an ex and gotten away with it.

☐ true ☐ false | ☐ true ☐ false

My favorite thing that one of my exes used to do is:

_____

_____

My least favorite thing that one of my exes used to do is:

_____

_____

When I was a teenager, I'd date people whom . . .

my parents liked	☐	☐
my parents disliked	☐	☐

I lost my virginity . . .

in high school	☐	☐
in college	☐	☐
after leaving school	☐	☐
before high school	☐	☐
hasn't happened yet	☐	☐

I wish I'd . . .

waited longer to lose my virginity	☐	☐
lost it sooner	☐	☐
I'm happy about the timing	☐	☐

Losing my virginity was . . .

something I'd rather forget	☐	☐
good emotionally, but not physically	☐	☐
good physically, but not emotionally	☐	☐
pretty great all around	☐	☐

The best sex I've ever had was:

_____

_____

The worst sex I've ever had was:

_____

_____

The most interesting place I've had sex was:

_____

_____

The place I liked having sex the least was:

_____

_____

I've been physically abused by an ex.

☐ yes ☐ no | ☐ yes ☐ no

I've been emotionally abused by an ex.

☐ yes ☐ no | ☐ yes ☐ no

I have been in a relationship where I felt like
I was losing myself.

☐ yes ☐ no | ☐ yes ☐ no

Because:

_____

_____

_____

_____

I think I could have stopped that from happening by:

_____

_____

_____

_____

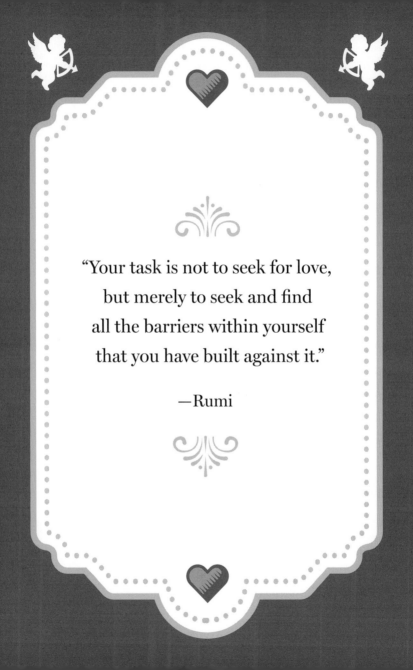

"Your task is not to seek for love,
but merely to seek and find
all the barriers within yourself
that you have built against it."

—Rumi

The one relationship mistake I never want to repeat:

_____

_____

_____

_____

One thing an ex did that made it harder for me to trust people:

_____

_____

_____

_____

One thing an ex did that made it easier for me to trust people:

_____

_____

_____

_____

My favorite thing about you that reminds me of
an ex:

_____

_____

My least favorite thing about you that reminds me
of an ex:

_____

_____

The ex I took the longest time getting over:

_____

_____

Because:

_____

_____

If I could go back in time and redo one thing from high school I'd:

_____

_____

_____

_____

If I could go back in time and redo one thing from college I'd:

_____

_____

_____

_____

If I had the choice to go back in time and say one thing I hadn't said or unsay one thing I had, I'd:

_____

_____

_____

_____

The biggest secret I hid under my bed as a teenager:

_____

_____

Hiding under my bed now:

_____

_____

My biggest regret:

_____

_____

_____

_____

One person I should have treated better:

_____

_____

The weirdest dream I've ever had:

_____

_____

_____

_____

My most embarrassing experience as a kid:

_____

_____

_____

_____

My most embarrassing experience as an adult:

_____

_____

_____

_____

Beliefs, Rituals, and Superstitions

Astrology is . . .

important ☐ interesting ☐ silly fun ☐ stupid ☐
important ☐ interesting ☐ silly fun ☐ stupid ☐

Tarot is . . .

important ☐ interesting ☐ silly fun ☐ stupid ☐
important ☐ interesting ☐ silly fun ☐ stupid ☐

Psychics are . . .

important ☐ interesting ☐ silly fun ☐ stupid ☐
important ☐ interesting ☐ silly fun ☐ stupid ☐

Friday the 13th is . . .

a sign of impending doom ☐ a little creepy
☐ just a movie ☐ just another day

a sign of impending doom ☐ a little creepy
☐ just a movie ☐ just another day

A broken mirror is . . .

a sign of impending doom □ a little creepy
□ just broken glass

a sign of impending doom □ a little creepy
□ just broken glass

Opening an umbrella indoors is . . .

bad luck □ harmless □

bad luck □ harmless □

Black cats are . . .

omens of bad luck □ adorable! □

omens of bad luck □ adorable! □

Witchcraft is . . .

a powerful skill set □ something I'd like to learn
more about □ phooey □

a powerful skill set □ something I'd like to learn
more about □ phooey □

Knock on wood and . . .

you'll have good luck □ you'll make a racket □

you'll have good luck □ you'll make a racket □

My Wisdom

The most important thing I learned about relationships in high school:

_____

_____

The most important thing I learned about relationships in my twenties:

_____

_____

The most important thing I've learned about relationships in the past year:

_____

_____

The most important thing I've learned about relationships with my current partner:

_____

_____

_____

_____

The most important thing I've learned about relationships while I've been alone:

_____

_____

_____

_____

The most important thing I've learned from a past hurt:

_____

_____

_____

_____

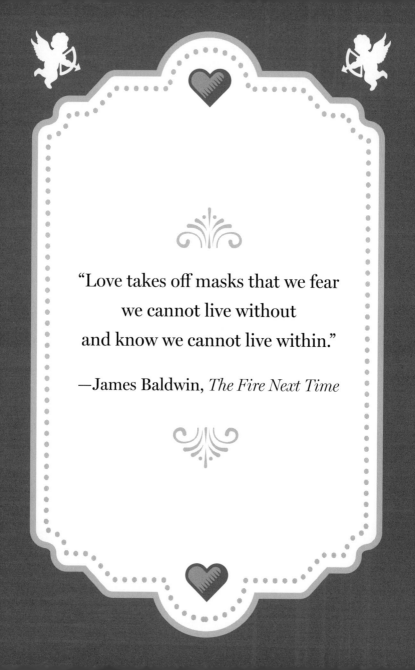

"Love takes off masks that we fear
we cannot live without
and know we cannot live within."

—James Baldwin, *The Fire Next Time*

The most important thing I've learned about families:

_____

_____

_____

_____

The most important thing I've learned about arguments:

_____

_____

_____

_____

The most important thing I've learned about sex:

_____

_____

_____

_____

The most important thing I've learned about
attraction:

_____

_____

_____

_____

The most important thing I've learned about you:

_____

_____

_____

_____

The most important thing I've learned about
myself:

_____

_____

_____

_____

The best relationship advice I've ever given:

_____

_____

_____

_____

The best relationship advice I've ever gotten:

_____

_____

_____

_____

The area in which I feel like I still have the most to learn:

_____

_____

_____

_____

CHAPTER 6

My Future

N ext up: Assessing your personal goals and how they align (or diverge) as a couple. How do you see your career progressing and how does your partner fit in the picture? Do you expect a spouse to stay home with kids, manage finances, handle household chores— or vice-versa? Whether you fit together like puzzle pieces, require negotiations, or hit a roadblock, these questions will certainly yield some interesting discussion.

My Career

It's okay for me to put my career ahead of my partner.

always	☐	☐
sometimes	☐	☐
never	☐	☐

It's okay for my partner's career to take precedence over me.

always	☐	☐
sometimes	☐	☐
never	☐	☐

I'm willing to support my partner while he or she goes through school.

☐ yes ☐ no | ☐ yes ☐ no

I'd prefer my partner to . . .

be in the same field as me	☐	☐
understand the field that I'm in	☐	☐
be in a completely different field than me	☐	☐

I'm willing to drop my career to raise kids.

yes, for a while	☐	☐
yes, permanently	☐	☐
no	☐	☐
career?	☐	☐

I expect my partner to drop his or her career
to raise kids.

☐ yes ☐ no | ☐ yes ☐ no

I feel like you take my career seriously.

true, and that's good	☐	☐
true, and that's bad	☐	☐
false, and that's good	☐	☐
false, and that's bad	☐	☐

I feel like you think my job is . . .

as important as yours	☐	☐
more important than yours	☐	☐
less important than yours	☐	☐

When it comes to my career . . .

I'm right where I want to be	☐	☐
I don't know what I want to do when I grow up	☐	☐
I feel pressured to move faster	☐	☐
I'm just doing this until something better comes along	☐	☐
I feel like I'm ahead of the game	☐	☐
I'd rather not work at all	☐	☐

If I won the lottery I'd . . .

stop working altogether	☐	☐
keep my job	☐	☐
keep my line of work but start a new business	☐	☐
launch a whole new career	☐	☐

I'll know I'm a success when:

_____

_____

_____

_____

If I could drop my current job and pursue any career at all, I'd:

_____

_____

_____

_____

The thing you could do that would be most helpful to my career would be:

_____

_____

_____

_____

In one year, I plan to be:

_____

_____

In five years, I plan to be:

_____

_____

In ten years, I plan to be:

_____

_____

In twenty years, I plan to be:

_____

_____

Hope is the thing with feathers

Emily Dickinson

Hope is the thing with feathers
That perches in the soul,
And sings the tune without the words,
And never stops at all,

And sweetest in the gale is heard;
And sore must be the storm
That could abash the little bird
That kept so many warm.

I've heard it in the chillest land,
And on the strangest sea;
Yet, never, in extremity,
It asked a crumb of me.

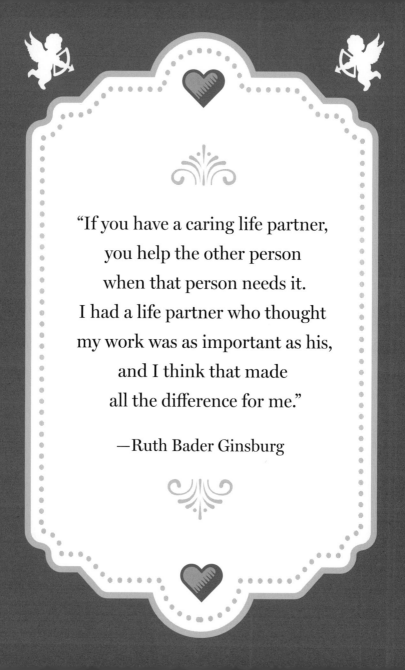

"If you have a caring life partner,
you help the other person
when that person needs it.
I had a life partner who thought
my work was as important as his,
and I think that made
all the difference for me."

—Ruth Bader Ginsburg

The difference between my career plans and my career dreams is:

_____

_____

Here's how you can help me lessen that difference:

_____

_____

The thing I like least about my job right now is:

_____

_____

The thing I like best about my job right now is:

_____

_____

Couple's C♥-purchase

Big-ticket co-purchases are an important step in a new relationship. Here's a list of possessions and how I'd prefer to handle payment and ownership between us:

car

solo ☐   together ☐   who needs it? ☐
solo ☐   together ☐   who needs it? ☐

washing machine

solo ☐   together ☐   who needs it? ☐
solo ☐   together ☐   who needs it? ☐

furniture

solo ☐   together ☐   who needs it? ☐
solo ☐   together ☐   who needs it? ☐

pet

solo ☐   together ☐   who needs it? ☐
solo ☐   together ☐   who needs it? ☐

vacation

solo ☐   together ☐   who needs it? ☐
solo ☐   together ☐   who needs it? ☐

air conditioner

solo ☐   together ☐   who needs it? ☐
solo ☐   together ☐   who needs it? ☐

cookware

solo ☐   together ☐   who needs it? ☐
solo ☐   together ☐   who needs it? ☐

exercise bike

solo ☐   together ☐   who needs it? ☐
solo ☐   together ☐   who needs it? ☐

spa trip

solo ☐   together ☐   who needs it? ☐
solo ☐   together ☐   who needs it? ☐

apartment or house

solo ☐   together ☐   who needs it? ☐
solo ☐   together ☐   who needs it? ☐

television

solo ☐   together ☐   who needs it? ☐
solo ☐   together ☐   who needs it? ☐

dishwasher

solo ☐   together ☐   who needs it? ☐
solo ☐   together ☐   who needs it? ☐

My Home

I expect that . . .

I'll be the disciplinarian	☐	☐
you'll be the disciplinarian	☐	☐
we'll share the job	☐	☐

I think it's okay to physically punish kids.

yes	☐	☐
only in extreme cases, such as slapping something dangerous out of a child's hand	☐	☐
never	☐	☐

I expect any kids we have to be raised . . .

within my specific branch of my faith	☐	☐
with a religious foundation	☐	☐
as agnostics	☐	☐
as atheists	☐	☐

I expect that . . .

you'll have the final say	☐	☐
I'll have the final say	☐	☐
we'll negotiate everything as a pair	☐	☐
you'll always have the final word in some areas, I'll always have it in others	☐	☐

I expect that . . .

you'll pay the bills	☐	☐
I'll pay the bills	☐	☐
we'll pay them together	☐	☐

My home needs to be . . .

immaculate	☐	☐
tidy	☐	☐
pleasantly cluttered	☐	☐
cleaned by others	☐	☐

If I had to choose one, I'd like my home to look . . .

perfect, like a magazine	☐	☐
lived-in	☐	☐

My best roommate

_____

_____

Because:

_____

_____

My worst roommate:

_____

_____

Because:

_____

_____

I expect that household repairs or building projects will be . . .

done by you	☐	☐
done by me	☐	☐
done by the two of us	☐	☐
done by skilled professionals	☐	☐

If there is a spider in the bathtub . . .

you squash it	☐	☐
I squash it	☐	☐
you put it outside	☐	☐
I put it outside	☐	☐
what's the big deal?	☐	☐
please don't ever make me think about spiders in the bathtub	☐	☐

I have fixed a part of my home with the proper tools.

☐ true ☐ false | ☐ true ☐ false

I'm like MacGyver with household problems.
I just need a fork, a bobby pin, or some other
surprisingly useful object.

☐ true ☐ false | ☐ true ☐ false

Love's Philosophy

Percy Bysshe Shelley

I

The fountains mingle with the river
And the rivers with the Ocean,
The winds of Heaven mix for ever
With a sweet emotion;
Nothing in the world is single;
All things by a law divine
In one spirit meet and mingle.
Why not I with thine?—

II

See the mountains kiss high Heaven
And the waves clasp one another;
No sister-flower would be forgiven
If it disdained its brother;
And the sunlight clasps the earth
And the moonbeams kiss the sea:
What is all this sweet work worth
If thou kiss not me?

My favorite thing about my home is:

_____

_____

My favorite piece of furniture is:

_____

_____

If I could change one thing about my home, I'd:

_____

_____

Here's how I think my home reflects my personality:

_____

_____

My favorite decoration in my home is:

_____

_____

_____

_____

My favorite smell to have in my home is:

_____

_____

_____

_____

If I could choose my perfect view, it would be:

_____

_____

_____

_____

House Hunting

When the time comes to move, my priorities
on choosing a neighborhood and home are as
follows (ranked from 1 to 15):

affordability ____ ____

size ____ ____

geographic location ____ ____

school quality ____ ____

demographics ____ ____

access to parks ____ ____

style of home ____ ____

state of construction ____ ____

parking ____ ____

neighborhood safety ____ ____

number of bathrooms ____ ____

sunlight ____ ____

convenience to amenities like
banks, restaurants, markets, etc. ____ ____

walkability ____ ____

commute time ____ ____

CHAPTER 7

Day by Day

If you're already spending tons of time together, you may know your partner's basic daily routines, habits, and quirks. But how do you *really feel* about those routines, habits, and quirks? And do you know how *they* feel about *yours*? It's time to lay it all on the table! The following questions cover day-to-day happenings, friends and family, and finances.

My Basics

I need to hear "I love you" every day.

☐ yes ☐ no | ☐ yes ☐ no

I like to have pet names for each other.

☐ yes ☐ no | ☐ yes ☐ no

I'm comfortable with public displays of affection.

☐ yes ☐ no | ☐ yes ☐ no

I'd prefer you to introduce me as your ...

girlfriend/boyfriend	☐	☐
friend	☐	☐
lover	☐	☐
reason for living	☐	☐

The most you should tell your friends about our sex life is ...

that it exists	☐	☐
that we're dating	☐	☐
tell them everything	☐	☐
tell them nothing	☐	☐

Calling each other at work to whisper sweet and/or filthy nothings is . . .

childish	☐	☐
fun	☐	☐
unprofessional	☐	☐
a good way to add spice	☐	☐

The most intense public display of affection I'm comfortable with is . . .

holding hands	☐	☐
a peck on the cheek	☐	☐
a closed-mouth kiss on the lips	☐	☐
deep kissing	☐	☐
heavy petting	☐	☐
I haven't found my limit yet	☐	☐
I'd prefer it if we just winked at each other	☐	☐

It's important to have moments of silence when we're together.

definitely ☐ ☐
are you kidding me? ☐ ☐

I expect to spend big chunks of time with you . . .

daily ☐ ☐
weekly ☐ ☐
every now and then ☐ ☐

I'm comfortable taking separate vacations:

once or twice ☐ ☐
a few times a year ☐ ☐
any time ☐ ☐
never ☐ ☐

How much time together is too much?

_____

_____

_____

_____

Solo or Together

Everybody needs space from time to time. Here are some activities I like to enjoy alone versus others I'd prefer to enjoy with you.

Exercising
solo ☐ together ☐ | solo ☐ together ☐

Seeing a movie
solo ☐ together ☐ | solo ☐ together ☐

Doing a crossword puzzle
solo ☐ together ☐ | solo ☐ together ☐

Reading
solo ☐ together ☐ | solo ☐ together ☐

Going to a concert
solo ☐ together ☐ | solo ☐ together ☐

Attending a work party
solo ☐ together ☐ | solo ☐ together ☐

Relationship quizzes
solo ☐ together ☐ | solo ☐ together ☐

Creative projects
solo ☐ together ☐ | solo ☐ together ☐

Clothes shopping
solo ☐ together ☐ | solo ☐ together ☐

"But let there be spaces
in your togetherness,
and let the winds of the heavens
dance between you.
Love one another
but make not a bond of love:
let it rather be a moving sea
between the shores of your souls."

—Kahlil Gibran

An evening in which we're both in the same
room but doing different things is . . .

perfect	☐	☐
comfortable	☐	☐
a sign that the relationship is in trouble	☐	☐

I sleep best . . .

alone	☐	☐
when you're there, but on your own side	☐	☐
when we're spooning	☐	☐
in a great big tangle, possibly with a cat or dog thrown in	☐	☐

I'm fine with eating dinner in front of the television.

☐ yes ☐ no ☐ sometimes

☐ yes ☐ no ☐ sometimes

I'm fine eating meals separately:

☐ yes ☐ no ☐ sometimes

☐ yes ☐ no ☐ sometimes

Food is . . .

one of life's sensual pleasures	☐	☐
workout fuel	☐	☐
a holistic way to nourish and heal your body	☐	☐
whatever is in the fridge	☐	☐

If one of us has dietary restrictions and one does not . . .

all meals cooked by either of us should follow those restrictions	☐	☐
the one with the restrictions follows them when cooking, the other does not	☐	☐
the one with the restrictions should occasionally cook food that she or he can't or won't eat	☐	☐

If one of us is vegetarian and one of us is not, it is okay for the carnivore to keep beef jerky in the house.

☐ yes ☐ no | ☐ yes ☐ no

If at least one of us is a vegetarian, it is okay to feed house pets foods that involve meat.

☐ yes ☐ no | ☐ yes ☐ no

If you're going to be out with your friends, I need you to call me and let me know where you are . . .

always	☐	☐
only if you need to change plans with me	☐	☐
only if you're going to be out late	☐	☐
never	☐	☐

If you make plans for a night that's usually a date night, I need to be informed . . .

as soon as possible	☐	☐
sometime that day	☐	☐
not at all; I don't assume we have plans until we've made them	☐	☐

If you need to change plans we've made, I need to be told . . .

a week before	☐	☐
at least a few hours before	☐	☐
ten minutes before	☐	☐

It's okay for you to say that both of us will be going to a party without checking with me first.

☐ yes ☐ no ☐ it depends on the event
☐ yes ☐ no ☐ it depends on the event

When I'm sad, I need to be . . .

cheered up   ☐   ☐
held   ☐   ☐
commiserated with   ☐   ☐
left alone   ☐   ☐

Complaining about something that
doesn't directly involve you means . . .

I want you to solve it   ☐   ☐
I just need to vent   ☐   ☐

Swearing is . . .

okay, as long as it's not in public
or in mixed company   ☐   ☐
never acceptable   ☐   ☐
acceptable if you save it for times
when you're genuinely upset   ☐   ☐
fucking great   ☐   ☐

A long-distance relationship . . .

is out of the question	☐	☐
would be difficult, but I could handle it	☐	☐
is something I could do, but only for a year or less	☐	☐
is something I could do, but only for six months or less	☐	☐
sounds ideal	☐	☐

If it's one of the last two options above, here's what I think that says about our relationship:

_____

_____

If you want to see a movie that I don't, and I want to see a movie that you don't, I expect that we will . . .

see both movies together	☐	☐
see our own movies separately	☐	☐
it's more likely that we'll both see yours and not mine	☐	☐
it's more likely that we'll both see mine and not yours	☐	☐

Pets sleeping in bed with us is . . .

disgusting ☐ ☐

cozy ☐ ☐

mandatory ☐ ☐

Pets should be . . .

free to roam the house ☐ ☐
restricted to certain rooms ☐ ☐
prohibited from certain pieces
of furniture ☐ ☐

Dogs should be . . .

big and goofy ☐ ☐

big and fierce ☐ ☐

medium-sized ☐ ☐

easily concealed in the
average purse ☐ ☐

purebred ☐ ☐

mutt ☐ ☐

hypoallergenic ☐ ☐

rescues ☐ ☐

Early to bed and early to rise makes a person . . .

healthy, wealthy, and wise	☐	☐
irritating	☐	☐

Breakfast should be:

just coffee	☐	☐
a quick bite of cereal or yogurt	☐	☐
protein for my workout	☐	☐
eggs, bacon, pancakes, the works!	☐	☐

Spicy foods:

the spice of life!	☐	☐
too harsh	☐	☐

Scooping out the chocolate chunks in the ice cream, leaving vanilla with little tunnels in it is:

perfectly acceptable	☐	☐
evil beyond all comprehension	☐	☐

Finishing the Oreos without replacing them or letting me know is:

perfectly acceptable	☐	☐
evil beyond all comprehension	☐	☐

In the car, I want to hear:

silence ☐ ☐
us talking ☐ ☐
NPR/the news ☐ ☐
talk radio ☐ ☐
sports ☐ ☐
rock ☐ ☐
hip-hop ☐ ☐
pop ☐ ☐
country ☐ ☐
classical ☐ ☐
jazz ☐ ☐
books on tape ☐ ☐

The maximum acceptable amount
of TV watching per week is:

unlimited ☐ ☐
anything under 20 hours ☐ ☐
anything under 10 hours ☐ ☐
anything under 5 hours ☐ ☐

Following a TV series is:

exciting and fun	☐	☐
a waste of time	☐	☐

Talking about movies is:

interesting	☐	☐
a waste of time	☐	☐

Talking about movie stars is:

interesting	☐	☐
a waste of time	☐	☐

Talking about sports is:

interesting	☐	☐
kill me	☐	☐

Competing against you at games or sports is:

fun	☐	☐
okay, sometimes	☐	☐
a bad idea	☐	☐

Compatibility
Potp♥urri

If I had to pick just one, I'd take:

rock	☐	☐
country	☐	☐
Star Wars	☐	☐
The Matrix	☐	☐
train	☐	☐
airplane	☐	☐
fiction	☐	☐
nonfiction	☐	☐
Dr. Seuss	☐	☐
Dr. Ruth	☐	☐
steak	☐	☐
ice cream	☐	☐
crossword puzzle	☐	☐
word search	☐	☐
Paris	☐	☐
Grand Canyon	☐	☐
Gone with the Wind	☐	☐
Fifty Shades of Grey	☐	☐
mayonnaise	☐	☐
mustard	☐	☐
hot sauce	☐	☐

As a rule, I expect to have sex . . .

at least once a day	☐	☐
at least once a week	☐	☐
at least once or twice a month	☐	☐
at least once during the course of our relationship	☐	☐

During sex, the lights should be . . .

on	☐	☐
off	☐	☐
natural sunlight	☐	☐
strobes and disco balls	☐	☐
let's mix it up	☐	☐

When it comes to positions . . .

I'm strictly missionary	☐	☐
I prefer to be on top	☐	☐
I like to switch it up for variety every now and then	☐	☐
I expect to discover at least six things that never made it into the *Kama Sutra*	☐	☐

I enjoy quickies.

☐ yes ☐ no | ☐ yes ☐ no

After sex, I like to:

cuddle	☐	☐
sleep	☐	☐
shower	☐	☐
watch TV	☐	☐
talk	☐	☐
other	☐	☐

It's okay to wake me up for sex.

always	☐	☐
never	☐	☐
sometimes	☐	☐
rarely	☐	☐

Sex should most often be:

tender and comforting	☐	☐
passionate and wild	☐	☐

[*Again and again, even though we know love's landscape*]

Rainer Maria Rilke

*Again and again, however we know the landscape of love
and the little churchyard there, with its sorrowing names,
and the frighteningly silent abyss into which the others
fall: again and again the two of us walk out together
under the ancient trees, lie down again and again
among the flowers, face to face with the sky.*

My Friends and Family

I expect you to know the names of and basic information about my friends.

no ☐ ☐
only my closest circle ☐ ☐
all of them ☐ ☐

I expect you to know the names of
and basic information about . . .

my parents ☐ ☐
my parents and siblings ☐ ☐
parents, siblings, grandparents, and cousins ☐ ☐
we're getting into second and
third cousins, so brace yourself ☐ ☐

The idea of having sex with you in
my parents' house over a holiday is . . .

naughty fun ☐ ☐
ordinary ☐ ☐
never speak of it again ☐ ☐

The member of my family I get along best with is:

_____

_____

The member of my family I most want *you* to get along with is:

_____

_____

The member of my family I think I'm most like is:

_____

_____

The member of my family I'd most like to improve my relationship with is:

_____

_____

I have . . .

a few close friends   ☐   ☐

lots of acquaintances   ☐   ☐

I've turned down dates because of my friends.

☐ true ☐ false | ☐ true ☐ false

I've dumped someone because of my friends.

☐ true ☐ false | ☐ true ☐ false

I've dated someone because of my friends

☐ true ☐ false | ☐ true ☐ false

I've stolen a mate from a friend.

☐ true ☐ false | ☐ true ☐ false

I've had a friend steal a mate from me.

☐ true ☐ false | ☐ true ☐ false

I've dated a friend's ex.

☐ true ☐ false | ☐ true ☐ false

I've dated a friend's ex behind their back.

☐ true ☐ false | ☐ true ☐ false

My best friend:

_____

_____

My best opposite-sex friend (if different):

_____

_____

The friend who is the worst influence on me:

_____

_____

The friend I most admire:

_____

_____

The first friend I'd call in a crisis:

_____

_____

The friend I'd want on my side in a physical fight:

_____

_____

The friend with the juiciest secrets:

_____

_____

The friend I'd most like to trade lives with:

_____

_____

The friend I'd never trade lives with:

_____

_____

The friend I most wish I'd kept in touch with:

_____

_____

The friend I'm most competitive with:

_____

_____

The friend I think you're most attracted to:

_____

_____

The friend I think is most likely to make a pass at you:

_____

_____

The friend you are most irrationally jealous of:

_____

_____

The friend I'm secretly attracted to:

_____

_____

If I had to marry one of my best friends I'd choose:

_____

_____

Because:

_____

_____

The worst friendship breakup I've had was:

_____

_____

The most touching thing a friend ever did for me was:

_____

_____

Three things I see in my friends' relationships that I hope won't happen to us:

1. _____

2. _____

3. _____

1. _____

2. _____

3. _____

Three things I envy about my friends' relationships:

1. _____

2. _____

3. _____

1. _____

2. _____

3. _____

My Finances

I expect:

my partner to take care of me	☐	☐
to take care of my partner	☐	☐
to trade off, depending on who's doing well	☐	☐

I'm in debt.

no way	☐	☐
a little	☐	☐
a lot	☐	☐
I'm drowning	☐	☐

It's okay for my partner to be in debt.

yes, unreservedly	☐	☐
yes, for things like student loans	☐	☐
depends on the partner, the kind, and the amount	☐	☐
not at all	☐	☐

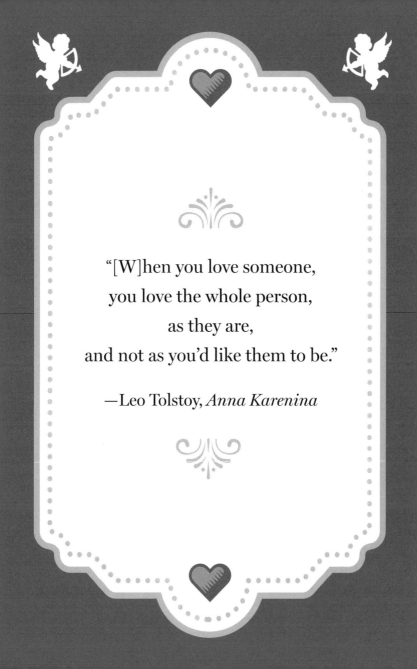

"[W]hen you love someone,
you love the whole person,
as they are,
and not as you'd like them to be."

—Leo Tolstoy, *Anna Karenina*

Once we're married or living together, I expect
us to have . . .

separate bank accounts	☐	☐
joint bank accounts	☐	☐
your account, my account, and our account	☐	☐

I'd prefer . . .

for you to take a strong interest in my finances	☐	☐
for you to have a general idea of how I'm getting along	☐	☐
for each of us to just take care of our own	☐	☐

Prenuptial agreements are:

smart planning	☐	☐
appalling	☐	☐

Making major purchases without telling
each other is . . .

okay	☐	☐
not okay	☐	☐

I expect to be . . .

richer than my parents	☐	☐
less well-off than my parents	☐	☐
about the same	☐	☐

I expect that . . .

I will make more money	☐	☐
you will make more money	☐	☐
it will be about the same	☐	☐
I will make all the money	☐	☐
you will make all the money	☐	☐

In all honesty, I would lose a little respect for my
partner if I were the bigger breadwinner.

☐ true ☐ false | ☐ true ☐ false

I'm a . . .

saver	☐	☐
spender	☐	☐
it feels like a pretty even balance	☐	☐

Ideally, I feel like I should be paired with a . . .

saver	☐	☐
spender	☐	☐
it doesn't matter	☐	☐

I feel like I'm prepared for retirement.

yes	☐	☐
no	☐	☐
I've done some planning, but could do more	☐	☐
what?	☐	☐

My Quirks

Love me, love my pet.

negotiable	☐	☐
nonnegotiable	☐	☐

Being alone is:

something I need so I can recharge	☐	☐
horrible	☐	☐

Household chores should be:

divided between us	☐	☐
my responsibility, as I'm better at them and have the time	☐	☐
your responsibility	☐	☐

I need to be able to sleep on "my" side of the bed.

☐ yes ☐ no | ☐ yes ☐ no

My living space needs to be . . .

immaculate	☐	☐
tidy, but not pristine	☐	☐
cluttered, but sanitary	☐	☐
left alone	☐	☐

Tidying my stuff away for me would be . . .

helpful	☐	☐
a violation	☐	☐
not something I'd notice	☐	☐

The toothpaste tube should be:

squeezed from the bottom and rolled up carefully	☐	☐
grabbed and squeezed from the middle	☐	☐
toothpaste?	☐	☐

I care about whether the toilet paper
rolls over or under.

☐ yes ☐ no | ☐ yes ☐ no

I have eliminated someone as a potential date
because of a bad voicemail.

☐ yes ☐ no | ☐ yes ☐ no

A Glimpse

Walt Whitman

A glimpse through an interstice caught,
Of a crowd of workmen and drivers in a bar-room
*   around the stove late of a winter night, and I*
*   unremark'd seated in a corner,*
Of a youth who loves me and whom I love, silently
*   approaching and seating himself near, that he may*
*   hold me by the hand,*
A long while amid the noises of coming and going, of
*   drinking and oath and smutty jest,*
There we two, content, happy in being together,
*   speaking little, perhaps not a word.*

C♥habitation: Chores I Hate vs. Chores I'll Tolerate

Are we compatible roommates? Dividing up household chores calls for compromise, so here's a list of chores I absolutely hate alongside chores I'd tolerate.

Washing dishes
hate ☐ tolerate ☐ | hate ☐ tolerate ☐

Laundry
hate ☐ tolerate ☐ | hate ☐ tolerate ☐

Organizing closets/drawers
hate ☐ tolerate ☐ | hate ☐ tolerate ☐

Cleaning the toilet
hate ☐ tolerate ☐ | hate ☐ tolerate ☐

Unclogging the toilet
hate ☐ tolerate ☐ | hate ☐ tolerate ☐

Changing the litter box
hate ☐ tolerate ☐ | hate ☐ tolerate ☐

Walking the dog
hate ☐ tolerate ☐ | hate ☐ tolerate ☐

Feeding pets
hate ☐ tolerate ☐ | hate ☐ tolerate ☐

Scrubbing/mopping floors
hate ☐   tolerate ☐ | hate ☐   tolerate ☐

Vacuuming
hate ☐   tolerate ☐ | hate ☐   tolerate ☐

Making the beds
hate ☐   tolerate ☐ | hate ☐   tolerate ☐

Cleaning the coffeepot
hate ☐   tolerate ☐ | hate ☐   tolerate ☐

Opening mail
hate ☐   tolerate ☐ | hate ☐   tolerate ☐

Cleaning the oven
hate ☐   tolerate ☐ | hate ☐   tolerate ☐

Purging the fridge
hate ☐   tolerate ☐ | hate ☐   tolerate ☐

Changing the bedding
hate ☐   tolerate ☐ | hate ☐   tolerate ☐

Paying the bills
hate ☐   tolerate ☐ | hate ☐   tolerate ☐

Grocery shopping
hate ☐   tolerate ☐ | hate ☐   tolerate ☐

Emptying the dishwasher
hate ☐   tolerate ☐ | hate ☐   tolerate ☐

Emptying trash
hate ☐   tolerate ☐ | hate ☐   tolerate ☐

Three things I suspect might bug you about me:

1. _____

2. _____

3. _____

1. _____

2. _____

3. _____

My top three pet peeves:

1. _____

2. _____

3. _____

1. _____

2. _____

3. _____

I think it's rude when people:

_____

_____

_____

_____

My favorite thing is when I notice people:

_____

_____

_____

_____

My favorite little courtesy:

_____

_____

_____

_____

Three things I pretend I like more than I actually do:

1. _____

_____

2. _____

_____

3. _____

_____

1. _____

_____

2. _____

_____

3. _____

_____

Three things I pretend I like less than I actually do:

1. _____

_____

2. _____

_____

3. _____

_____

1. _____

_____

2. _____

_____

3. _____

_____

Traveling T♥gether

My top priorities when planning a trip,
ranked from 1 to 20:

affordable accommodations   ___ ___

cosmopolitan location   ___ ___

free WiFi   ___ ___

cultural offerings like museums
and tours   ___ ___

world-famous restaurants   ___ ___

interesting cuisines and street food   ___ ___

beaches, lakes, and any swimming
opportunities   ___ ___

proximity to friends and family   ___ ___

shopping   ___ ___

avoiding language barriers   ___ ___

peace and quiet   ___ ___

excellent photo possibilities   ___ ___

bars, clubs, or live music scenes   ___ ___

adventure/outdoor sports   ___ ___

free tours and activity options   ___ ___

beautiful landscapes like mountains,
volcanoes, and canyons   ___ ___

Before we go on a trip, I need to . . .

Map out our itinerary	☐	☐
Book the best restaurants	☐	☐
Plan our travel budget	☐	☐
Do nothing but pack a duffle bag and hit the road!	☐	☐

With a long flight ahead, I plan to . . .

Nap	☐	☐
Read	☐	☐
Watch a movie	☐	☐
Chat with you	☐	☐
Chat with our neighbors	☐	☐

My vacation days begin . . .

Bright and early	☐	☐
After sleeping in	☐	☐
With a raging hangover	☐	☐
When the clubs open	☐	☐

Once we're at our destination, my preferred
mode of transportation is . . .

the local metro	☐	☐
walking	☐	☐
a Vespa scooter or motorcycle	☐	☐
Uber	☐	☐
transportion? I'll be sleeping by the pool	☐	☐

Most of my travel budget will be spent on . . .

hotels	☐	☐
meals	☐	☐
souvenirs	☐	☐
museums and historical sights	☐	☐
bars and nightclubs	☐	☐

If the forecast says rain showers all day, I would . . .

Stay in our hotel and watch TV	☐	☐
Go to the bar	☐	☐
Read a book	☐	☐
Hit a casino	☐	☐
Pop on my raincoat and see the sights	☐	☐

My vacation photo album is mostly . . .

couple's selfies	☐	☐
beautiful landscapes and sunsets	☐	☐
local color and street scenes	☐	☐
you in front of cultural sights	☐	☐
me in front of cultural sights	☐	☐
every meal we enjoyed	☐	☐

If I get sick on vacation, I expect you to . . .

Stay by my side until I'm ready for action	☐	☐
Go out and enjoy yourself as planned	☐	☐

CHAPTER 8

My Body

From personal grooming to diet and exercise to confidence in the bedroom, how you take care of yourself and how you feel about your body can both have an impact on your relationship. In this chapter, you'll share your preferences, turn-ons, and hang-ups to get your bodily rhythms in sync.

Care and Feeding

Working out is . . .

my life	☐	☐
something I do, but dislike	☐	☐
something I avoid at all costs	☐	☐

Yoga is:

good for the body	☐	☐
good for the body, mind, and spirit	☐	☐
no good	☐	☐

Plastic surgery is:

creepy	☐	☐
a miracle	☐	☐

For me, personal grooming is . . .

the basics—a shower and a touch-up	☐	☐
my favorite part of the day	☐	☐
something I'll go all-out on for special occasions	☐	☐
an hour in the bathroom every morning, minimum	☐	☐

I prefer my underarms . . .

shaved	☐	☐
natural	☐	☐

I prefer my legs . . .

shaved	☐	☐
natural	☐	☐

I prefer to keep my pubic region . . .

natural	☐	☐
trimmed	☐	☐
partially shaved or waxed	☐	☐
bare	☐	☐

If you have a different preference . . .

I'll keep it the way you like it best	☐	☐
we can discuss it, depending on what you want	☐	☐
you should think about whether that's a dealbreaker for you	☐	☐

Good-Night

Percy Bysshe Shelley

Good-night? ah! no; the hour is ill
Which severs those it should unite;
Let us remain together still,
  Then it will be good night.

How can I call the lone night good,
Though thy sweet wishes wing its flight?
Be it not said, thought, understood,
Then it will be good night.

To hearts which near each other move
From evening close to morning light,
The night is good; because, my love,
They never say good-night.

Grooming
& Self-Care

Choose one:

□ □ bar soap | □ □ body wash

□ □ electric toothbrush | □ □ regular toothbrush

□ □ perfume/cologne | □ □ scented lotion | □ □ au natural

□ □ brush | □ □ comb

□ □ soap and water | □ □ hand sanitizer

□ □ dental floss | □ □ toothpick

□ □ nail scissors | □ □ nail clippers | □ □ nail file

□ □ shaving | □ □ waxing | □ □ au natural

□ □ manicure | □ □ pedicure | □ □ neither

□ □ foot massage | □ □ back massage | □ □ neck massage

□ □ acupuncture | □ □ aromatherapy

□ □ meditation | □ □ medication

□ □ beard | □ □ mustache | □ □ clean-shaven

□ □ makeup | □ □ the natural look

□ □ glass of wine | □ □ cup of tea

I consider myself . . .

a vegetarian	☐	☐
a carnivore	☐	☐
a vegan	☐	☐
health-conscious	☐	☐
can't people just be quiet and eat?	☐	☐

I have dietary restrictions . . .

due to my religion	☐	☐
due to allergies or a health issue	☐	☐
due to moral issues	☐	☐
for weight control	☐	☐
my diet is only restricted by the capacity of my stomach	☐	☐

I can live with someone who has dietary restrictions that are different from mine . . .

unreservedly	☐	☐
begrudgingly	☐	☐
if they're for health reasons	☐	☐
if they're for religious or moral reasons	☐	☐
actually, I can't	☐	☐

Mind over Matter

My favorite body part is:

_____

_____

My least favorite body part is:

_____

_____

I think I look best when I'm:

_____

_____

I feel sexiest when I'm:

_____

_____

5 things I like about my body that most people are self-conscious about:

1. _____

2. _____

3. _____

4. _____

5. _____

1. _____

2. _____

3. _____

4. _____

5. _____

5 things I like about your body that you're self-conscious about:

1. _____

2. _____

3. _____

4. _____

5. _____

1. _____

2. _____

3. _____

4. _____

5. _____

Dancing makes me feel . . .

sexy   ☐   ☐

self-conscious   ☐   ☐

I think I'm . . .

great in bed   ☐   ☐

average in bed   ☐   ☐

in need of some practice and
maybe a manual or two   ☐   ☐

I don't like it when you touch my:

_____

_____

I love it when you touch my:

_____

_____

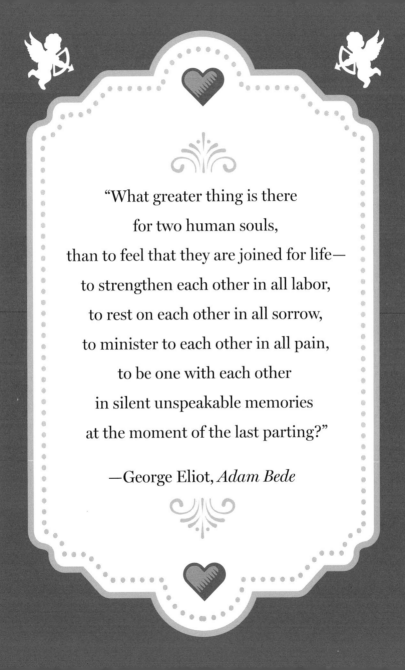

"What greater thing is there
for two human souls,
than to feel that they are joined for life—
to strengthen each other in all labor,
to rest on each other in all sorrow,
to minister to each other in all pain,
to be one with each other
in silent unspeakable memories
at the moment of the last parting?"

—George Eliot, *Adam Bede*

I think the sex symbol I'm most like is:

_____

_____

The sex symbol I've never understood the appeal
of is:

_____

_____

Here's the advantage I have over him or her:

_____

_____

The sex symbol I'm most attracted to is:

_____

_____

The most attractive I've been in my life is:

_____

_____

I know I can always seduce you by:

_____

_____

I'm pretty sure I could seduce anyone by:

_____

_____

I forget to be self-conscious when I'm:

_____

_____

The best thing you could say to me before sex is:

_____

_____

_____

_____

The best thing you could say to me during sex is:

_____

_____

_____

_____

The best thing you could say to me after sex is:

_____

_____

_____

_____

Sleeping P♥siti♥ns

Sharing a bed comfortably can take time (and some maneuvering). Here are my preferred co-sleeping positions, ranked from 1 to 15.

spoon	___	___
loose spoon (without full body contact)	___	___
face to face	___	___
back to back	___	___
entwined	___	___
nuzzled (with my head on your chest or vice-versa)	___	___
on opposite ends of the bed	___	___
mirror image	___	___
fetal position	___	___
foot touch	___	___
hand hold	___	___
flat on stomach	___	___
flat on back	___	___
we both do our own thing	___	___
separate beds	___	___

CHAPTER 9

Fighting Words

All couples have to navigate rough waters in their relationship from time to time, and how you handle disagreements and full-blown fights can say a great deal about the longevity and health of your relationship. Luckily, anyone can learn how to resolve disagreements with mutual respect and understanding—all it takes is honest communication and a little work.

In the Heat of the Moment

Fights are . . .

best avoided at all costs	☐	☐
exciting	☐	☐
scary	☐	☐
over the minute one of us shouts	☐	☐
a useful way to hash out issues	☐	☐
no holds barred	☐	☐

A couple that never fights is . . .

happy	☐	☐
suppressing things	☐	☐

Going to bed angry:

never	☐	☐
sometimes you just have to	☐	☐

All fights need to be resolved
before they're dropped.

☐ yes ☐ no | ☐ yes ☐ no

If you ask me if something is wrong and I say "nothing," I really want you to . . .

pursue me and dig a little deeper	☐	☐
leave me alone while I think about it	☐	☐
believe me when I say that there's nothing wrong	☐	☐

If I'm upset about something, I need to talk about it . . .

right now	☐	☐
after I've cooled down	☐	☐

I prefer to discuss problems in our relationship . . .

face to face	☐	☐
while we're doing something else, like taking a walk	☐	☐
with someone else first	☐	☐

Things you say to me during the course of an argument are . . .

brushed off the minute we're done	☐	☐
going to keep hurting for a while	☐	☐

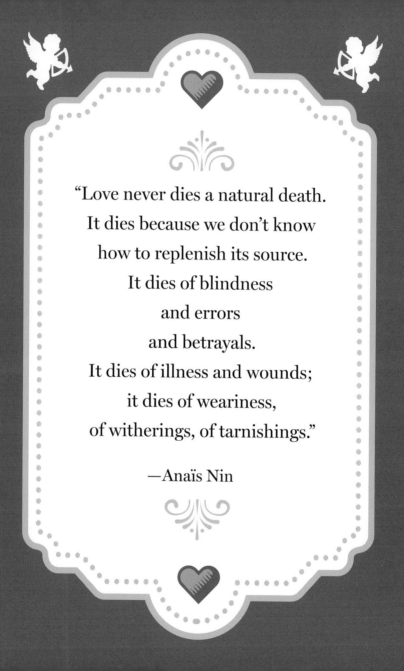

"Love never dies a natural death.
It dies because we don't know
how to replenish its source.
It dies of blindness
and errors
and betrayals.
It dies of illness and wounds;
it dies of weariness,
of witherings, of tarnishings."

—Anaïs Nin

A fight about doing the dishes is . . .

probably about doing the dishes	☐	☐
probably about something else	☐	☐

Bringing up past arguments in a current fight is . . .

fair	☐	☐
unfair	☐	☐

Taking a break in the middle of a fight to cool down is . . .

a good idea	☐	☐
not something I can do	☐	☐

After a fight, I need to . . .

be apart for a while	☐	☐
connect with you right away, to know we're okay	☐	☐

In the end, I expect . . .

one of us to win the fight	☐	☐
the two of us to compromise	☐	☐

We fight . . .

more than I did in most past relationships	☐	☐
less than I did in most past relationships	☐	☐
about the same	☐	☐

Relationship counselors . . .

help couples argue more productively	☐	☐
don't help	☐	☐

Talking to friends about our fights is . . .

☐ okay ☐ not okay | ☐ okay ☐ not okay

You have hit a level of anger that
frightened me in the past.

☐ yes ☐ no | ☐ yes ☐ no

I have hit a level of anger that
frightened me in the past.

☐ yes ☐ no | ☐ yes ☐ no

I think we resolve conflicts:

☐ well ☐ badly | ☐ well ☐ badly

The thing you do during arguments that I find unfair is:

_____

_____

The thing I do during arguments that is probably unfair is:

_____

_____

I wish you had more of a sense of humor about:

_____

_____

That said, I am never going to have a sense of humor about:

_____

_____

The thing you do during arguments that I find unfair is:

_____

_____

The dumbest fight we've had was about:

_____

_____

The fight that was best for our relationship was:

_____

_____

The one fight I'd love to remove from our lives together is:

_____

_____

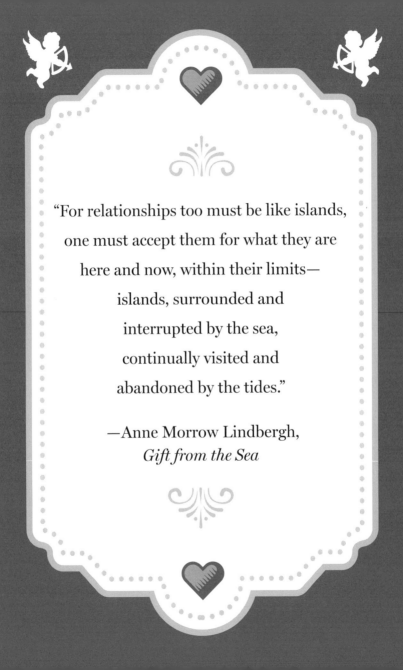

"For relationships too must be like islands, one must accept them for what they are here and now, within their limits— islands, surrounded and interrupted by the sea, continually visited and abandoned by the tides."

—Anne Morrow Lindbergh, *Gift from the Sea*

Brutally Honest

Really, honestly, truly—relationship drama is . . .

something I can't stand ☐ ☐

something I might secretly
enjoy a little bit ☐ ☐

my lifeblood ☐ ☐

I am able to admit it when I'm in the wrong.

☐ yes ☐ no ☐ yes, but usually not right away

☐ yes ☐ no ☐ yes, but usually not right away

Makeup sex:

no such thing ☐ ☐

depends on the fight ☐ ☐

the whole reason for having the
argument in the first place ☐ ☐

Withholding sex to get my way is . . .

fair ☐ ☐

unfair ☐ ☐

unfair, but I'll do it if it's something
important to me ☐ ☐

I'm used to winning arguments.

☐ true ☐ false | ☐ true ☐ false

I'm likely to say something I don't mean in a fight.

☐ true ☐ false | ☐ true ☐ false

I've resorted to emotional blackmail before.

☐ true ☐ false | ☐ true ☐ false

I've lied to win arguments or smooth over
conflicts in the past.

☐ true ☐ false | ☐ true ☐ false

I've been gaslighted in the past.

☐ true ☐ false | ☐ true ☐ false

I have gaslighted others in the past.

☐ true ☐ false | ☐ true ☐ false

Once a conflict is resolved, I generally
don't hold grudges.

☐ true ☐ false | ☐ true ☐ false

The Limits of
My Devoti♥n

I would do anything for love, but I won't do this:

Karaoke
I'd do it ☐   absolutely not ☐   maybe ☐
I'd do it ☐   absolutely not ☐   maybe ☐

Go vegan
I'd do it ☐   absolutely not ☐   maybe ☐
I'd do it ☐   absolutely not ☐   maybe ☐

Dispose of a body
I'd do it ☐   absolutely not ☐   maybe ☐
I'd do it ☐   absolutely not ☐   maybe ☐

Have a threesome
I'd do it ☐   absolutely not ☐   maybe ☐
I'd do it ☐   absolutely not ☐   maybe ☐

Square dancing
I'd do it ☐   absolutely not ☐   maybe ☐
I'd do it ☐   absolutely not ☐   maybe ☐

Lie to your mom
I'd do it ☐   absolutely not ☐   maybe ☐
I'd do it ☐   absolutely not ☐   maybe ☐

Quit alcohol and/or smoking

I'd do it ☐   absolutely not ☐   maybe ☐

I'd do it ☐   absolutely not ☐   maybe ☐

Move cities

I'd do it ☐   absolutely not ☐   maybe ☐

I'd do it ☐   absolutely not ☐   maybe ☐

Donate an organ

I'd do it ☐   absolutely not ☐   maybe ☐

I'd do it ☐   absolutely not ☐   maybe ☐

Go to dinner with your horrible boss

I'd do it ☐   absolutely not ☐   maybe ☐

I'd do it ☐   absolutely not ☐   maybe ☐

Lie to get out of a party

I'd do it ☐   absolutely not ☐   maybe ☐

I'd do it ☐   absolutely not ☐   maybe ☐

Get matching tattoos

I'd do it ☐   absolutely not ☐   maybe ☐

I'd do it ☐   absolutely not ☐   maybe ☐

Shave my head

I'd do it ☐   absolutely not ☐   maybe ☐

I'd do it ☐   absolutely not ☐   maybe ☐

CHAPTER 10

Breaking Up

It might feel uncomfortable to discuss past breakups with a new partner, but speaking honestly about your experiences (whether amicable, contentious, or tragic) can also deepen the understanding between you and ultimately bring you closer. Those lessons learned, openly discussed, and applied to your current relationship will set a foundation of trust and honesty that's essential in any healthy coupling.

Water Under the Bridge

Breakups should happen:

in person	☐	☐
on the phone	☐	☐
via text message	☐	☐
just "ghost" and stop responding to calls and texts	☐	☐

Breaking up in a restaurant or other public place in the hopes that the other person won't make a scene:

effective	☐	☐
cowardly	☐	☐
humiliating	☐	☐

I have more often been . . .

the one who gets dumped	☐	☐
the one who does the dumping	☐	☐
it's about even	☐	☐

In the past, I have threatened to break up . . .

in the heat of an argument	☐	☐
if it's an issue that's really	☐	☐
important to me	☐	☐
only when I am actually prepared to walk out the door	☐	☐
I don't threaten, I do it	☐	☐

In the past, I've waited until I found a new partner before breaking up with the old one.

☐ true ☐ false | ☐ true ☐ false

I've sabotaged or broken off a relationship to avoid a difficult conversation.

☐ true ☐ false | ☐ true ☐ false

I've sabotaged or broken off a relationship because it got too serious for me.

☐ true ☐ false | ☐ true ☐ false

The one thing I couldn't stand about my worst breakup was:

_____

_____

_____

_____

The thing I most appreciated a partner doing in a past breakup was:

_____

_____

_____

_____

The thing I'm proudest of in handling a past breakup:

_____

_____

_____

_____

The worst thing I did in a past breakup:

_____

_____

_____

_____

The thing that worries me most about your past
breakups:

_____

_____

_____

_____

A lesson I've learned from past breakups that I hope
to bring to our relationship

_____

_____

_____

_____

A Little too Close for Comfort

I've thought about leaving our relationship.

□ true □ false | □ true □ false

Because:

_____

_____

I ended up staying because:

_____

_____

If we ever break up, I expect it to be because of:

_____

_____

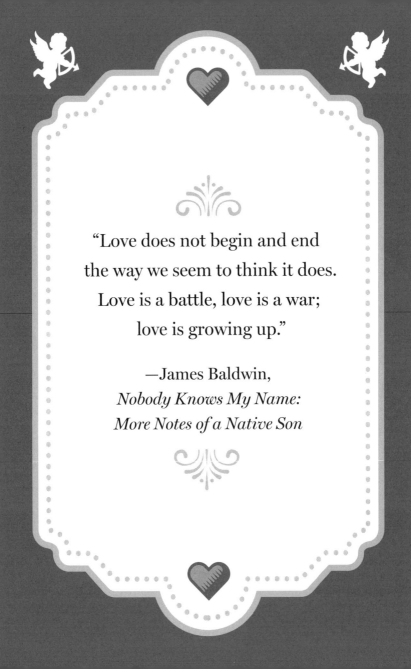

"Love does not begin and end
the way we seem to think it does.
Love is a battle, love is a war;
love is growing up."

—James Baldwin,
*Nobody Knows My Name:
More Notes of a Native Son*

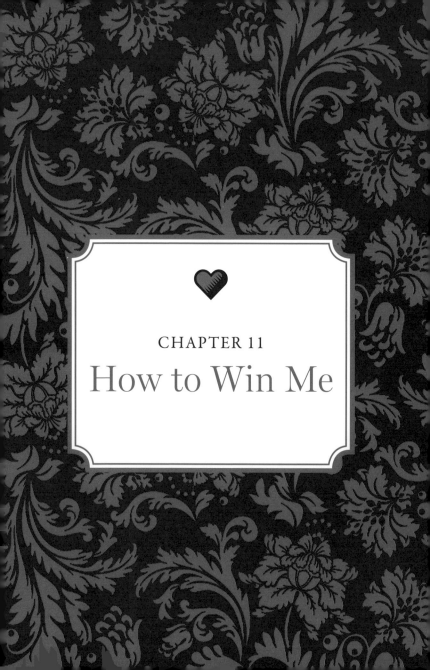

CHAPTER 11

How to Win Me

If you've been together awhile, you might feel that you've already wooed and won. Not so fast: Seduction is an art, yes, but it's also a skill that takes forethought and practice. How well do you know your partner's turn-ons and desires? The following questions will be enlightening for new couples and a refresher for long-term lovers—either way, they'll bring a little spice to your everyday.

The Chase

I'd rather . . .

be pursued	☐	☐
do the pursuing	☐	☐

Someone who is openly attracted to me is . . .

an aphrodisiac	☐	☐
too easy	☐	☐

I'd rather have you . . .

seduce me with your eyes from across the room	☐	☐
slam me into a wall and kiss me hard	☐	☐

I prefer . . .

to know you're making an effort to charm me	☐	☐
for you to be absolutely real with me	☐	☐

I'm intrigued by people who challenge me.

☐ yes ☐ no | ☐ yes ☐ no

Witty banter:

is the spice of life	☐	☐
requires too much thought	☐	☐

Tickling:

love it	☐	☐
hate it	☐	☐
not ticklish	☐	☐

Teasing me:

love it	☐	☐
hate it	☐	☐

Teasing me in bed:

love it	☐	☐
hate it	☐	☐

I still enjoy a high school–style makeout
in the back of a car.

☐ true ☐ false | ☐ true ☐ false

A bubble bath for two sounds . . .

sensual ☐ ☐

crowded ☐ ☐

Soft music and candlelight is . . .

romantic ☐ ☐

boring ☐ ☐

fun to try ☐ ☐

Foot rubs are . . .

good ☐ ☐

weird ☐ ☐

best when they lead to something more ☐ ☐

I'd rather . . .

be the boss ☐ ☐

be dominated a little bit ☐ ☐

switch roles ☐ ☐

Staring into each others' eyes during sex is:

intimate ☐ ☐

creepy ☐ ☐

My Dream Lunch Date

Choose one:

☐ ☐ Michael Jordan | ☐ ☐ Tom Brady

☐ ☐ Barack Obama | ☐ ☐ George W. Bush

☐ ☐ Cher | ☐ ☐ Madonna

☐ ☐ Stephen King | ☐ ☐ Michael Crichton

☐ ☐ Ruth Bader Ginsburg | ☐ ☐ Clarence Thomas

☐ ☐ Mark Zuckerberg | ☐ ☐ Elon Musk

☐ ☐ Don Draper | ☐ ☐ Tony Soprano

☐ ☐ Meryl Streep | ☐ ☐ Miley Cyrus

☐ ☐ Bowie | ☐ ☐ Jagger

☐ ☐ Tina Belcher | ☐ ☐ Lisa Simpson |
☐ ☐ Daria Morgendorffer

☐ ☐ Winston Churchill | ☐ ☐ Franklin D. Roosevelt

☐ ☐ Jay Gatsby | ☐ ☐ Atticus Finch

☐ ☐ The Kardashians | ☐ ☐ The Windsors

☐ ☐ Ellen DeGeneres | ☐ ☐ Whoopi Goldberg

"Bright star, would I were stedfast as thou art"

John Keats

Bright star, would I were stedfast as thou art—
Not in lone splendour hung aloft the night
And watching, with eternal lids apart,
Like nature's patient, sleepless Eremite,
The moving waters at their priestlike task
Of pure ablution round earth's human shores,
Or gazing on the new soft-fallen mask
Of snow upon the mountains and the moors—
No—yet still stedfast, still unchangeable,
Pillow'd upon my fair love's ripening breast,
To feel for ever its soft fall and swell,
Awake for ever in a sweet unrest,
Still, still to hear her tender-taken breath,
And so live ever—or else swoon to death.

The Cold Hard Truth

In all honesty, physical attractiveness is . . .

irrelevant ☐ ☐
a nice icing on the cake ☐ ☐
something that makes me a little wary ☐ ☐
one way to attract me ☐ ☐
the main thing I look for ☐ ☐
essential ☐ ☐

In all honesty, sexual prowess is . . .

essential ☐ ☐
icing on the cake ☐ ☐
a little too much pressure ☐ ☐

In all honesty, if you stop chasing me . . .

we can relax ☐ ☐
I'll leave ☐ ☐

In all honesty, a little danger in the relationship is . . .

essential ☐ ☐
going to drive me away eventually ☐ ☐

In all honesty, making me a little jealous is
a good way to keep me interested.

☐ true ☐ false | ☐ true ☐ false

In all honesty, I tend to be more attracted to people
who don't quite treat me well.

☐ true ☐ false ☐ true, but I'm trying to
break the habit

☐ true ☐ false ☐ true, but I'm trying to
break the habit

In all honesty, sending me mixed signals . . .

turns me off	☐	☐
intrigues me	☐	☐

In all honesty, I'm really only fully attracted to . . .

someone who takes on a strong masculine role	☐	☐
someone who takes on a strong feminine role	☐	☐
someone who completely rejects traditional masculinity	☐	☐
someone who completely rejects traditional femininity	☐	☐
someone who's a little androgynous	☐	☐
I'm flexible	☐	☐

Compatibility
Potp♥urri

If I had to pick just one, I'd take:

voicemail	☐	☐
text message	☐	☐
pretzels	☐	☐
potato chips	☐	☐
James Joyce	☐	☐
James Patterson	☐	☐
unicorns	☐	☐
narwals	☐	☐
horror	☐	☐
tragedy	☐	☐
religion	☐	☐
spirituality	☐	☐
A Christmas Carol	☐	☐
The Nutcracker	☐	☐
cable TV	☐	☐
Netflix	☐	☐
broccoli	☐	☐
Brussels sprouts	☐	☐
Friends	☐	☐
Seinfeld	☐	☐

Spoil Me a Little

Surprises make me feel . . .

happy and excited	☐	☐
anxious and out of control	☐	☐

Giving me a romantic card "just because" is . . .

sweet	☐	☐
sappy	☐	☐

A nice massage . . .

puts me to sleep	☐	☐
turns me on	☐	☐
there is no such thing as a nice massage	☐	☐

Breakfast in bed should be . . .

eggs and sausage	☐	☐
pancakes	☐	☐
fresh berries and cream	☐	☐
all of those	☐	☐
avoided until I've had a chance to wash my face and brush my teeth	☐	☐

Lingerie is . . .

really a gift for me	☐	☐
really a gift for you	☐	☐

Giving me a book as a present is . . .

thoughtful	☐	☐
good, depending on the book	☐	☐
the same as giving me a doorstop	☐	☐

Lotions and bath salts are . . .

in the way	☐	☐
luxurious	☐	☐

A single rose is . . .

the perfect romantic gesture	☐	☐
where are the rest of them?	☐	☐

Writing me a poem or song is . . .

incredibly romantic	☐	☐
sweet, but not my thing	☐	☐

Surprising me after work with a movie rental
and some takeout is . . .

a relaxing treat	☐	☐
a little too much like our usual routine	☐	☐

The best thing you can do for me after
I've had a hard day at work is . . .

cook me dinner	☐	☐
give me a back rub	☐	☐
leave me alone for a while	☐	☐
give me a hug	☐	☐
let me talk about it	☐	☐

If you were to cook (or buy) me a meal, I'd like:

_____

_____

_____

_____

Aedh Wishes for the Cloths of Heaven

William Butler Yeats

Had I the heavens' embroidered cloths,
Enwrought with golden and silver light,
The blue and the dim and the dark cloths
Of night and light and the half-light,
I would spread the cloths under your feet:
But I, being poor, have only my dreams;
I have spread my dreams under your feet;
Tread softly because you tread on my dreams.

My birthday is . . .

something I prefer to ignore	☐	☐
something I celebrate privately	☐	☐
a great excuse to go out drinking with friends	☐	☐
a night for a party and cake	☐	☐
a ME day	☐	☐

Birthday and holiday presents should be . . .

practical	☐	☐
fun	☐	☐
romantic	☐	☐
complete surprises	☐	☐

It's okay to give me a birthday gift that's really for my child or my pet.

☐ true ☐ false | ☐ true ☐ false

I think that Valentine's Day is . . .

romantic	☐	☐
silly, but fun	☐	☐
something we should ignore	☐	☐
mandatory	☐	☐

Flowers or Valentine presents
delivered to my office are . . .

fun, but unnecessary	☐	☐
embarrassing	☐	☐
a sweet gesture	☐	☐
a way to rack up major points	☐	☐

Let's agree to give each other gifts for . . .

birthdays and major holidays only	☐	☐
all the holidays!	☐	☐

I keep a running list of gift ideas for you.

☐ true ☐ false | ☐ true ☐ false

If you gave me an unexpected gift for no reason,
I would probably . . .

feel embarrassed and plan to
reciprocate ☐ ☐

appreciate it but would not feel
the need to reciprocate ☐ ☐

If I gave you an expensive watch while you gave me a
handmade card, I would be . . .

disappointed that I spent more than you ☐ ☐

moved by the thoughtful and
creative gesture ☐ ☐

If you gave me an expensive watch while I gave
you a handmade card, I would be . . .

embarrassed for not splurging too ☐ ☐
proud of my thoughtful gesture ☐ ☐

Here are my sizes for future clothing purchases:

shirts _____ _____ pants _____ _____
dresses _____ _____ shoes _____ _____
jackets _____ _____
ring size (wink wink) _____ _____
don't even think about it _____ _____

Spoil Big

The perfect weekend morning for me is . . .

work	☐	☐
going to religious services	☐	☐
a quiet breakfast in bed	☐	☐
reading the paper, cover to cover	☐	☐
yoga, a bike ride, or a hike at sunrise	☐	☐
over before I wake up	☐	☐

Public displays such as having musicians in a restaurant come over to serenade me are . . .

wonderful!	☐	☐
embarrassing, but fun	☐	☐
will drive me under the table	☐	☐

The idea of a whole night dedicated just to my pleasure . . .

makes me nervous	☐	☐
makes me feel selfish	☐	☐
sounds wonderful if I can reciprocate later	☐	☐
sounds perfect	☐	☐

H♥t Dates

Here's how I'd rank the following date ideas, from 1 to 15.

Picnic on the beach   ____   ____

Making sushi at home   ____   ____

Wine tasting   ____   ____

Karaoke   ____   ____

Couples' massage   ____   ____

Bike ride   ____   ____

Hiking   ____   ____

Brewery tour   ____   ____

Baseball game   ____   ____

Pub trivia   ____   ____

Pot luck party   ____   ____

Camping weekend   ____   ____

Bowling   ____   ____

Art museum   ____   ____

Poetry reading   ____   ____

Netflix and chill   ____   ____

A vacation to me means . . .

lots of physical activity	☐	☐
lots of relaxing	☐	☐

A camping trip sounds like . . .

a lot of fun	☐	☐
you're testing me and our relationship	☐	☐
most of my long weekends	☐	☐
pure hell	☐	☐

A weekend getaway should be . . .

just us	☐	☐
us and our friends	☐	☐

Giving me a spa day would . . .

make me feel pampered	☐	☐
make me feel like you think I need work	☐	☐

Assuming kids are in the picture, I'd prefer . . .

romantic vacations for two	☐	☐
family vacations	☐	☐

The perfect vacation spot for me would be . . .

any place with plenty of booze, clubs, and dancing	☐	☐
any place with a beach	☐	☐
international city, glamorous hotel, plenty of shopping	☐	☐
a cottage in the country	☐	☐
a tent in the woods	☐	☐
any place I can get some extreme sports in	☐	☐
backpacking through a country I've never been to	☐	☐
my place, with the phone turned off	☐	☐

If I could visit any country in the world, I'd choose:

_____

_____

_____

_____

Perfume is . . .

a good present because I want to wear a scent you like	☐	☐
not a good present unless you already know what I prefer to wear	☐	☐
a good present because you chose it for me	☐	☐
not a good present because I don't like perfume	☐	☐

Diamonds are . . .

a waste of money	☐	☐
a girl's best friend	☐	☐
immoral	☐	☐
pretty, but not necessary	☐	☐
something I'd enjoy	☐	☐

Should it come up, I'd rather . . .

be surprised with a ring	☐	☐
shop together	☐	☐

I've always dreamed of living in a:

penthouse apartment	☐	☐
castle	☐	☐
mansion	☐	☐
little house with a yard	☐	☐
igloo	☐	☐
tree house	☐	☐
yacht	☐	☐
other	☐	☐

It makes me feel special when you:

_____

_____

_____

_____

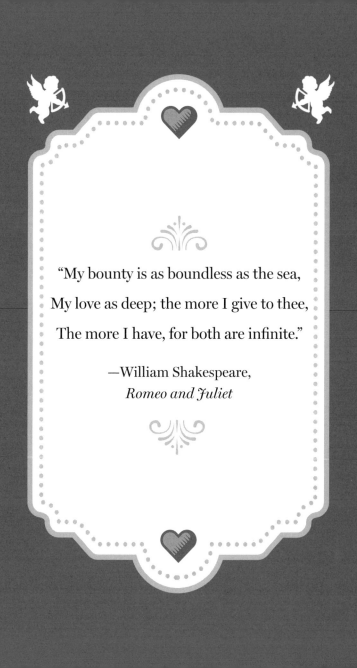

"My bounty is as boundless as the sea,
My love as deep; the more I give to thee,
The more I have, for both are infinite."

—William Shakespeare,
Romeo and Juliet

CHAPTER 12

More Things to
Love About Me

J ust when you think you know everything there is to know about your partner, buckle up. This chapter covers all the bits and bobs of your personalities, quirks, and inner thoughts—from guilty pleasures and pop culture favorites to personal embarrassments and secret fantasies.

My Likes and Dislikes

My top five favorite movies:

1. _____

2. _____

3. _____

4. _____

5. _____

1. _____

2. _____

3. _____

4. _____

5. _____

My favorite actor:

_____

_____

My favorite actress:

_____

_____

My favorite classy celebrity:

_____

_____

My favorite trashy celebrity:

_____

_____

My favorite television show:

_____

_____

My favorite guilty television pleasure:

_____

_____

My favorite comedian/comedienne:

_____

_____

My favorite TV personality:

_____

_____

My favorite author:

My favorite book:

My favorite children's book:

My favorite word:

Compatibility
Potp♥urri

If I had to pick just one, I'd take:

shot	☐	☐	John Waters	☐	☐
cocktail	☐	☐	John Wayne	☐	☐
wine	☐	☐			
beer	☐	☐	guacamole	☐	☐
			salsa	☐	☐
Lord of the Rings	☐	☐	queso	☐	☐
Harry Potter	☐	☐			
			paper	☐	☐
hot dogs	☐	☐	plastics	☐	☐
hamburgers	☐	☐	reusables	☐	☐
SnapChat	☐	☐	hardcover	☐	☐
WhatsApp	☐	☐	paperback	☐	☐
			ebook	☐	☐
Winnie the Pooh	☐	☐	audiobook	☐	☐
Paddington	☐	☐			
salt	☐	☐			
pepper	☐	☐			

Love's Trifling

Thomas Moore

If in loving, singing, night and day,
We could trifle merrily life away,
Like atoms dancing in the beam,
Like day-flies skimming o'er the stream,
Or summer-blossoms, born to sigh
Their sweetness out, and die,—
How brilliant, thoughtless, side by side,
Thou and I could make our minutes glide!
No atoms ever glanced so bright,
No day-flies ever danced so light,
Nor summer blossoms mixed their sigh
So close as thou and I!

My favorite sport to watch:

_____

_____

My favorite sport to play:

_____

_____

My favorite game that I'm good at:

_____

_____

My favorite game that I'm bad at:

_____

_____

My top five favorite bands or musicians:

1. _____

2. _____

3. _____

4. _____

5. _____

1. _____

2. _____

3. _____

4. _____

5. _____

My favorite song right now:

_____

_____

My favorite song of all time:

_____

_____

My favorite sad song:

_____

_____

My favorite love song:

_____

_____

My favorite karaoke song:

_____

_____

My favorite makeout song:

_____

_____

My favorite workout song:

_____

_____

My favorite album:

_____

_____

"[I]t's no good pretending
that any relationship has a future
if your record collections
disagree violently
or if your favorite films
wouldn't even speak to each other
if they met at a party."

—Nick Hornby, *High Fidelity*

My favorite smell:

_____

_____

My favorite food:

_____

_____

You're never going to get me to eat:

_____

_____

My favorite drink:

_____

_____

My favorite sound:

_____

_____

My favorite color:

_____

_____

My favorite season:

_____

_____

My favorite fabric:

_____

_____

My favorite gift I've received as an adult:

_____

_____

My favorite childhood gift:

_____

_____

My favorite thing I've made with my hands:

_____

_____

My favorite gift I've given to someone else:

_____

_____

My favorite body part on men:

_____

_____

My favorite body part on women:

_____

_____

The habit that drives me crazy:

_____

_____

A habit that I'll probably never give up:

_____

_____

My favorite city:

_____

_____

My favorite vacation spot:

_____

_____

The country I'd most like to live in:

_____

_____

The country I've been to that I'll never need
to see again:

_____

_____

My favorite way to travel:

road trip	☐	☐
plane	☐	☐
ocean liner	☐	☐
bike	☐	☐
there's no place like home	☐	☐

other:

_____

_____

My favorite kind of party:

swanky cocktails	☐	☐
dinner for six	☐	☐
plenty of friends, plenty of board games	☐	☐
loud music and sexy dancing	☐	☐

other:

_____

_____

My favorite night at the movies:

romance	☐	☐
suspense	☐	☐
comedy	☐	☐
action	☐	☐
horror	☐	☐
foreign	☐	☐
documentary	☐	☐
other:		

_____

_____

My favorite way to see live music:

from the moshpit	☐	☐
at a jazz club	☐	☐
in a ballroom	☐	☐
at an outdoor festival	☐	☐
at a honky-tonk	☐	☐
other:		

_____

_____

Inside My Head

Three things about me of which I'm proudest:

1. _____
   _____

2. _____
   _____

3. _____
   _____

1. _____
   _____

2. _____
   _____

3. _____
   _____

Three things about me that are the hardest to admit:

1. _____

   _____

2. _____

   _____

3. _____

   _____

1. _____

   _____

2. _____

   _____

3. _____

   _____

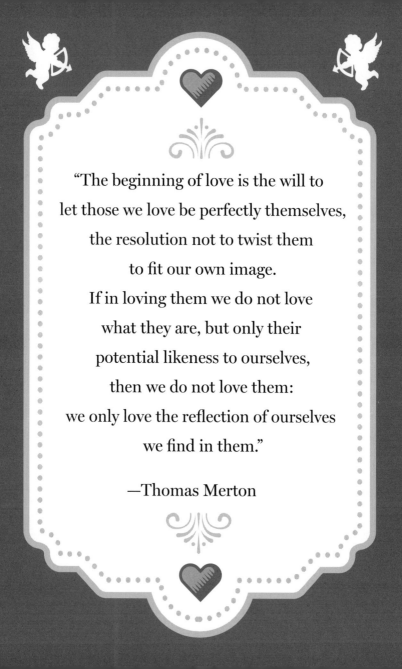

"The beginning of love is the will to
let those we love be perfectly themselves,
the resolution not to twist them
to fit our own image.
If in loving them we do not love
what they are, but only their
potential likeness to ourselves,
then we do not love them:
we only love the reflection of ourselves
we find in them."

—Thomas Merton

The best compliment I've ever received:

_____

_____

The weirdest compliment I've ever received:

_____

_____

The one thing that always turns me off is:

_____

_____

The quality I see in myself that I can't stand
in others is:

_____

_____

The fantasy or movie scene that's always secretly turned me on is:

_____

_____

The oldest person I've fantasized about:

_____

_____

The best dream I ever had is:

_____

_____

Before I met you, of course, the person I most often fantasized about was:

_____

_____

Making noise in bed . . .

adds spice	☐	☐
makes me worry we'll be overheard	☐	☐
makes me worry that I'll sound silly	☐	☐
is essential	☐	☐

I fantasize more about . . .

being rescued	☐	☐
doing the rescuing	☐	☐

I'd rather . . .

see something sexy	☐	☐
read something sexy	☐	☐
hear something sexy	☐	☐

I believe sexual orientation is . . .

fixed	☐	☐
fluid	☐	☐

To me, the sexiest professions are (check all that apply):

firefighter	☐	☐
doctor/nurse	☐	☐
mechanic	☐	☐
dancer	☐	☐
CEO	☐	☐
construction worker	☐	☐
lawyer	☐	☐
police officer	☐	☐
artist	☐	☐
international spy	☐	☐
actor	☐	☐
writer	☐	☐
scientist	☐	☐
politician	☐	☐
bartender	☐	☐
pilot	☐	☐
soldier	☐	☐
musician	☐	☐

other:

_____

_____

The girliest thing about me is:

_____

_____

_____

_____

The most masculine thing about me is:

_____

_____

_____

_____

If I could change one thing about the world
right now, I'd:

_____

_____

_____

_____

Just for Fun

I've always wished I were really good at:

_____

_____

The surefire way to make me laugh is to:

_____

_____

The surest way to tell that I'm happy is:

_____

_____

The best indication that I need some space is:

_____

_____

My weirdest celebrity crush is:

_____

_____

My inner animal is a:

_____

_____

If I were a kind of flower, I would be:

_____

_____

If I could choose my own nickname, I'd pick:

_____

_____

I think I'd have made a good . . .

royal	☐	☐
world leader	☐	☐
pirate	☐	☐
comedian	☐	☐
rock star	☐	☐
spy	☐	☐
actor	☐	☐
other:		

_____

_____

If I were a drink, I would be a . . .

soda	☐	☐
juice	☐	☐
beer	☐	☐
martini	☐	☐
white wine	☐	☐
red wine	☐	☐
gin and tonic	☐	☐
scotch	☐	☐
other:		

_____

_____

If I were making lunch or dinner to please my inner child, I'd make:

_____

_____

The fairy-tale character I most identify with:

_____

_____

My favorite real-life hero:

_____

_____

My favorite superhero:

_____

_____

Supreme Superher♥es

Here's how I'd rank the following superheroes,
from 1 to 20:

Batman   ____   ____

Black Widow   ____   ____

Blade   ____   ____

Buffy Summers   ____   ____

Captain America   ____   ____

Deadpool   ____   ____

Hancock   ____   ____

Hellboy   ____   ____

Hulk   ____   ____

Iron Man   ____   ____

Robocop   ____   ____

Scott Pilgrim   ____   ____

Storm   ____   ____

Superman   ____   ____

T'Challa   ____   ____

Thor   ____   ____

Valkyrie   ____   ____

Wolverine   ____   ____

Wonder Woman   ____   ____

Xena   ____   ____

The villain I secretly identify with:

_____

_____

The public figure I'm convinced is a real-life villain:

_____

_____

The era in history I'd most like to live in:

_____

_____

If I could go back in time and change one historical event, it would be:

_____

_____

I know it's not the height of fashion, but I love the way I look when I wear my:

_____

_____

The worst haircut I've ever had was:

_____

_____

The worst thing I personally have done:

_____

_____

My biggest fear:

_____

_____

If I could eradicate one disease, I'd knock out:

_____

_____

If I could have one superpower I'd choose:

_____

_____

If I could choose one micropower I'd choose:

always being able to find a parking space ☐ ☐

waking up on time without an alarm
clock ☐ ☐

a personal radius of perfect cell phone
reception ☐ ☐

other:

_____

_____

If I could be a genius at one art form I'd choose:

classical musician	☐	☐
rock star	☐	☐
jazz cat	☐	☐
painter	☐	☐
sculptor	☐	☐
architect	☐	☐
actor	☐	☐
singer	☐	☐
dancer	☐	☐
photographer	☐	☐
director	☐	☐
writer	☐	☐

other:

_____

_____

I'd rather win:

an Olympic medal	☐	☐
a Nobel Prize	☐	☐
the Pulitzer Prize	☐	☐
an Academy Award	☐	☐

I think the game show I'd be most likely to clean up on is:

_____

_____

A reality show about my life would be called:

_____

_____

In the movie of my life, I'd be played by:

_____

_____

If I were a sitcom character, I'd be on:

_____

_____

Compatibility
Potp♥urri

If I had to pick just one, I'd take:

more smarts	☐	☐
increased hotness	☐	☐
master thief	☐	☐
master sleuth	☐	☐
caviar	☐	☐
chili dog	☐	☐
Brad Pitt	☐	☐
Cary Grant	☐	☐
cheese	☐	☐
chocolate	☐	☐
Oscar Wilde	☐	☐
The Three Stooges	☐	☐
James Bond	☐	☐
Indiana Jones	☐	☐
fruit	☐	☐
vegetables	☐	☐
King Kong	☐	☐
Godzilla	☐	☐

red	☐	☐
black	☐	☐
Glinda the Good Witch	☐	☐
The Wicked Witch of the West	☐	☐
pirate	☐	☐
ninja	☐	☐
leather	☐	☐
lace	☐	☐
Broadway musical	☐	☐
basketball game	☐	☐
walking	☐	☐
sprinting	☐	☐
Abba	☐	☐
The Sex Pistols	☐	☐
music with a message	☐	☐
shut up and dance	☐	☐
Casino	☐	☐
The Big Lebowski	☐	☐
tattoos	☐	☐
piercings	☐	☐
Winnie the Pooh	☐	☐
Paddington	☐	☐

I am ...

a cat person	☐	☐
a dog person	☐	☐
a person who thinks it's ridiculous to try to divide the world into cat people and dog people	☐	☐
more into reptiles	☐	☐
not an animal lover	☐	☐

I think climate change is real:

☐ yes ☐ no | ☐ yes ☐ no

I believe in extraterrestrials:

☐ yes ☐ no | ☐ yes ☐ no

I'm excited about intergalactic possibilities:

☐ yes ☐ no | ☐ yes ☐ no

I believe in ghosts.

☐ yes ☐ no | ☐ yes ☐ no

I keep a diary.

☐ yes ☐ no | ☐ yes ☐ no

Night Thoughts

Johann Wolfgang von Goethe

Despite your beauty and your high estate,
Unhappy stars, I pity you your fate,
The roaming mariner who gladly guide,
Without reward, across the foaming tide:
For ye are not loved, neither do ye love!
Unceasingly in your career above
Ye move across the dark expanse of heaven;
And through what space ye have already driven,
While I have, by the side of love, of night,
And, hapless stars, of you, forgot the flight!

If I knew I could get away with it, the biggest crime I'd commit is:

_____

_____

The most high-maintenance thing I do is:

_____

_____

The possession I'd run into a burning building to save:

_____

_____

I'm embarrassed about this, but I'm really good at:

_____

_____

The coolest thing in my music collection:

_____

_____

The most embarrassing thing in my music collection:

_____

_____

One last awesome thing you need to know about me:

_____

_____

_____

_____

N♥tes

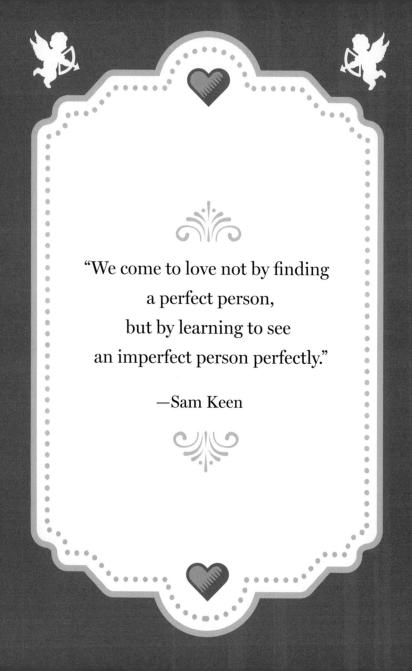

"We come to love not by finding
a perfect person,
but by learning to see
an imperfect person perfectly."

—Sam Keen

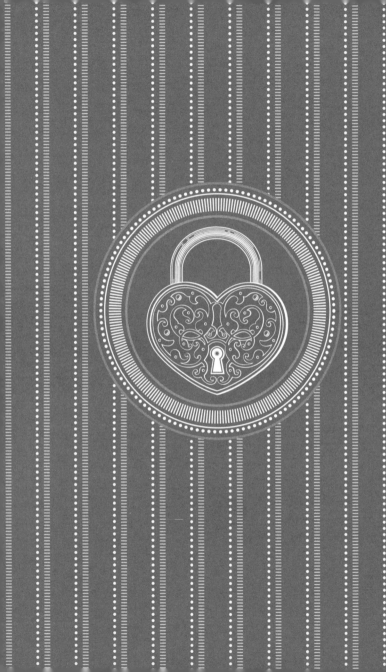